"I WAITED PATIENTLY FOR THE LORD; HE TURNED TO ME AND HEARD MY CRY. HE LIFTED ME OUT OF THE SLIMY PIT, OUT OF THE MUD AND MIRE; HE SET MY FEET ON A ROCK AND GAVE ME A FIRM PLACE TO STAND. HE PUT A NEW SONG IN MY MOUTH, A HYMN OF PRAISE TO OUR GOD. MANY WILL SEE AND FEAR AND PUT THEIR TRUST IN THE LORD...." PSALM 40:1-3

Dedications

"I am a living testimony. This book is not my story; it's my life. I dedicate this book to those of you who are still alive and are struggling to overcome the spirit of rejection, depression, bitterness and all forms of oppression. He (God) overcame so you (we) overcome. To my family, both near and far, you are my life-line; thank you for your place in my life. Whether you are my push or my pull, I need you and it's because of you that I have made it this far. To my mother, thank you for your sacrifices and love for me. I am your *Jewel*. I also dedicate this book to my father, the late Joseph Moore Jr. Thank you for my life; without you, there would be no *me*. Lastly mentioned, but not the least, to my Lord and Savior, Jesus Christ, who found a way to love me... you are my Life. Thank you, Father, for collecting all of my broken pieces, and putting *Jewel* together. If I had ten thousand tongues, I'd use just one of them to ask you for ten thousand more, just to sing your praises for the rest of my life. I dedicate this assignment to You, Father; it's through you, to you and with you, that this assignment was birthed. I love you."

TABLE OF CONTENTS

"How do You love ME?"

Collecting jewel's...

Introduction

To the young woman, searching for love because her father wasn't there to secure her with love...this book is for you. Young man, caught up in the system because your family system was broken...this book is for you. You may be the father, struggling to show love to your children because, nobody ever showed you how...this book is for you. If you're that single mother, secretly battling depression, while trying to raise your kids alone...this book is for you. Maybe you're that wife, struggling to cover your husband's heart because, your heart is bleeding; this book is for you. Perhaps you are the father, accused of walking out, but you don't know how to fix it...this book is for you. Maybe you're the father, left to care for the kids because your wife decided to move on; this book is for you. As for you...you may be the child, struggling to find your place, in the situation that you were born into...this book is for you. If you are human and you've had an encounter with love or hate, this book is for you.

"How do YOU love ME" is a piece of the author's heart. Both captivating and provocative, this book tells a story about the author's fight to win the victory over rejection and depression. The author, most known for her transparency, puts all of her cards on the table and provokes you to "play her hand." No matter what hand you were dealt in life, you are still set up to win...if you play your cards right. We don't know that we're fighters until we're put to the test; we don't know that...we don't have to fight until we discover we have a choice. Everyone is looking for love. Even if we are filled with hate, it's because we are angry with love. We want to know if we're loved or just how much. It's not always a verbal question; matter of fact, we don't think it's healthy to ask, but everyone, in everything that we do, wants to know, just how we're loved.

Word on the street

Poetically Speaking...

"I like to be clear...but we love the riddle games."

I don't mean to be vain but we all sit the same.

Now let me explain: I'm not always clear...and that's my fear. I want you to...want to...understand.

See, rejection is that "thing" that we see from one side of the track; we cry "rejection," at times, before we have all of the facts.

We want to be accepted even if we have the slack. Matter of fact, we lack the confidence it takes to speak up...still we want to be heard...but that's not a verb. We think in a much higher tone than the silent stones that we throw behind our tongues.

When we talk about "rejection" we're still talking about "love"... two adjectives...two verbs.

This is a "life-telling" conversation that I'd like to have with you; although I'll talk much more than you...not to be rude but from the horse's mouth flows the best truth.

Let's talk about Love; "How do You love ME?" I'll wait for your response, but please... let me speak..."

There is one thing that the whole world has in common. It's a part of who we are. It doesn't always have to be verbal and it doesn't always have to be obvious; even when we feel we've never seen it, we seek to find its true existence. We believe in it, even if we harbor hate. We're all talking about *love*. In this heart to heart, conversational piece, we will explore and reveal some truths about the word most talked about in some shape, form or fashion, at some point in all of our lives: we're all talking about *love*. Love is the purest four letter word known to man. We talk about love every day in everything that we do. We are human beings, created to *be*. We want to be needed, we want to be accepted, we want to be left alone at times, we want to be forgiven, we want to forgive and we need to be loved. Furthermore, we want it to all happen on our own terms. At the end of the day, we want to be understood if we express our desire for these "be's" all at the wrong time. We want acceptance but we feel we shouldn't have to ask for it, we want patience but we shouldn't have to wait for it. We need love, but we don't want to fight for it and this one can be tricky because we may put up a fight in the name of love, but beneath the surface, we're really fighting for our own pride and "deserved" respect. We don't want to be...rejected. We shape our lives to fit into something. We want to know if we're loved, but it's not genuine if we have to ask for it. Even when we're wrong, we expect to be loved and forgiven; no one has the right to hold a thing over anyone's head...right? Would that be love? If that's not love, would we call it hate? Even the most hateful person is STILL talking about love. From the rich to the poor, for better or for worst, we all desire to be loved the right way, but is *that* right? Who defines the expression of love? The proud man wants to know, "How could you *not* love me?" The guilty man wants to know, "Do you still love me?" The insecure man says: "How do YOU love ME?" When it's all said and done, the content man will shout, with a loud voice: "OH!! How you love me!"

Most people are not afraid of love; we are afraid of the sacrifices that come with it. We know that love will, quite naturally, take something from us and we're, at times, unwilling to run the risk of not getting that "something" back; furthermore, we don't know what love will take, borrow, use or lead us to give away. We fear experiencing love's splendor and then having it change its form right before our very own eyes...and God forbid if love changes when our eyes are *closed;* we fail to realize that even if love changes while our eyes are closed, we too grow in our sleep. We change, but we expect the expression of love to remain the same. Most people would rather not experience love at all than to have it fade away or taken from them JUST as they were getting comfortable. Everybody, everywhere, in everything is talking about love. So, let's talk about it together. Take this journey with me as I expose some encounters I've had with love in my own life as well as experiences with love, from its most rejected state, to its fullness, beauty and splendor.

L-O-V-E letters

       During our conversation, I hope to paint a picture for you. They say a picture is worth hundreds of words, but we're only talking about one word: *love.* Now, this is not a story, but life in its truest form… my life, your life, her life, his life, the life you chose, the life you've heard of, the life you've created, and for some, the life you can still avoid. Life is *life;* it defines itself. The definitiveness of life is found in its ability to be lived. Life happens to us all and we rejoice in this because anything outside of life would ultimately be the death of us all. Some live life to the fullest while others live most of their lives on empty waiting to be filled. Some say live life like it's your last day; I say live life like it's a gift and life's purpose has been fulfilled. Life makes *life* worth living. I once heard a person say, "I hate Mondays!" I'm never quick to judge, but we all decipher what we hear and think…is that not judging? Maybe it's not such a scary word after all but I digress. As for Monday's, there are so many who never got to see the Monday that turns your world upside down; if Monday never came for you, this would be the end of life as you know it.

       I'm a wordy person and words mean a lot to me. I'm not big on abbreviations though…they make us lazy, at times. We abbreviate words and things that would only take a millisecond longer to say or express if we just spelled them out. Don't get me wrong though; I don't hate them all, but what are we rushing for? It's my belief that some words are short enough to be spelled out while others are worth the extra time it takes to spell them out. There is nothing funnier to me than a *nick name* that's longer than the original name. Why abbreviate? Is life too short; is it too abbreviated? Maybe life is short, but the most trying moment can feel like a lifetime within itself. Cats may have nine lives, but people have many. Our lives can start again as long as we have the sense of smell. I know what you're thinking; "as long as I have breath in my body, I'm alive." That may be true. Since the beginning of time, the substance of life has been based on man's ability to inhale the breath of God; it is God who created man to be and God who sends the flood to flush out the bad, though some good gets lost in the flood. Nevertheless, it is He who restores the earth and starts life again. We assume that all we've lost in the journey were things that we didn't need anyway, and that's not always true. I think we say, "I must've not needed it anyway, if God took it," because we can't really explain why we had to lose something. It's the way we cope with the unexplainable. We are not comfortable with giving people this explanation: "I don't

x

know why I lost that thing, but God does and it's well with my soul." For example, a woman's long beautiful hair may be cut off just hours before a major brain surgery in efforts to get to her brain; the cut had little to do with the hair. The hair just happened to be the thing that covered an area that needed to be operated on so the hair had to be cut off, to get to the affected area; fortunately, most hair can and will grow back again…if not, she may learn that she is still beautiful without it. If all else fails, she will find that beautiful mole in the middle of her forehead really accents her eyes. If the hair grows back, it may not grow back the same way, same texture, color or length but it's still her hair. Will she worry though? Will she worry because people can't see the actual area of operation…they will only see where the hair has been cut off? If she's not careful, she too will become distracted by the loss of hair and fail to heal properly or fail to thank God for making it through the surgery that so many lost their lives in. Before you cry over her lost hair, let's think about our own personal losses. See, the reason for the hair being cut off is obvious but what if the "thing" that was cut off, was not so obvious? How do we process and explain it? Would you focus on the lost thing or the fact that you made it through? The fact that you are here, alive and able to read this book proves that you made it through something; I don't know how you made it or what you've gone through, but I know that you've made it. Even the homeless man, in Tuscaloosa, Al, sitting on the corner of McFarland Boulevard, who has been there for 20 years, begging for food, is an over comer. I know this because, a few years ago in Tuscaloosa, Al, a category five tornado came through and many lives were claimed; his life was obviously spared. We are still here and so is he but, how did we handle what we made it through? This is where the road divides most of us. We're not talking about Tuscaloosa and we're not talking about a homeless man; we're still talking about love. We love according to what's happened to us. See, some handle the *cuts* of life with grace while others are still praying for grace to make it through something that…God has already brought them through. They just can't live outside of what happened to them. Some things are so traumatizing for us that we live through them, but we are held hostage by the "details" of the thing we made it through. I survived the rape but can I live on, knowing that the rape was permitted…to happen to me? I survived but, it happened to me, so I love like, "Why me?" Let's go back to the example of the lady who has to shave her hair for surgery: Some of us would show up for our surgery with our heads already shaved; no doctor would have to tell us that we need to cut a little hair so that he could get to a particular area, on our heads. Now, although this would appear to be boldness, and would be for some, it could also indicate that we want to control the situation; some would show up with the hair already cut off, simply because they want to be the one doing the "cutting" if anyone is going to cut. Motive is key. On the other hand, we cut the hair ourselves because we genuinely want to make the "doctor's" job easier; we know the hair will get in the way of the surgical procedure. At times, we know that we need to let go of things and people so that we can sense God clearly in a situation and grow properly. For the rest of us, we negotiate with the physician; we inquire well ahead of time about the surgery because we want to know how much hair we will have to lose, question the notion of cutting the hair and offer ways to work around it. We don't like to lose things that make us feel secure; this reminds us of rejection. We don't like to be rejected. Some people argue that good things have a higher price to pay, yet we all believe that love shouldn't cost a thing. Some people believe love is what love does, but do we really know what love is supposed to do? Chronicles 28:9 tells us that, "The Lord searches every heart and understands every motive behind the thoughts. IF you seek him, he will be found by you; but if you forsake him, he will reject you forever." The Lord rejects…forever?? Wow! Don't cry just yet; let's take a closer look: In the bible, forever has proven to be a "not so long" time. "If my people who are called by my name will humble themselves and pray and seek my face and turn from their wicked ways, then I will hear from heaven, and I will forgive their sin and will heal their land." II Chronicle's 7:14. God's rejection cannot be defined by using the emotion attached to the world's injection of meaning. Some words have been associated with so much negative emotion that we take on a different posture just by hearing or seeing the word before it's ever used in a sentence. God's rejection has little to do with Him and is more of a choice for the person "being" rejected; we walk away and He remains in one place…consistently. What is rejection though and how does it make us feel? How do we associate the actual act of rejection with what we feel? Rejection makes us feel, "un-picked, not the best choice, there is something/someone better than you." Does rejection have anything to do with love? How valuable is your love? Do you charge people to love you? What is your price based on? How do you love? I know you want to answer, but please, let me speak.

A lot has changed since the beginning of time, but not quite as much as we think. Some things never change, but somehow, someway, things end up just how God created them to be. I've had my share of life, but still I live to sing about it. We all have a story but nobody's story is the same. We all have eyes, and even if we see the same picture, our mouths will testify of the same portrait... viewed from several different angles. Even if your story is the same as mine, you will probably tell it differently; our eyes are not the same. Some walk by faith and some walk by sight. I invite you to follow me as I paint a self-portrait of myself, though, in it, you may see someone else...maybe even you. Just for a while, look with me into my mirror as I reflect on some of the most trying times in my life; those trying times that pushed me right into the hands of love. Explore with me as I share my testimony about how I found rejection and love both at the same place and time. Along the way, we'll collect some jewels, but don't throw them away, if they don't shine the way you think they should. Some truths about me, may be hard to swallow but, nobody asked you to eat. We're just talking and we're still talking about love. Here we go.

First Love

  In the beginning, God created the heavens and God
created this earth; from the deep soil of the earth, He too created
Mississippi's finest cut stone: *Jewel.* Funny thing about jewelry
though, whose value increases over time: you can were it,
treasure it, sale it, buy it, repair it, display it, size it, mold it, or
chose to simply leave it in the store on the top shelf, behind the
counter and it will still hold its rooted DNA of a precious cut
stone. I make no apologies neither do I require the same. Every
bruise makes a beauty mark and stands strong over time. Let's
mark this date: February 28, 1982. This date is the birth of *Jewel.*
While Joe was singing, *Up where we belong*, Quarter flash was
singing, *Harden your heart.* Both of those songs are perfect for
the birth of Jewel. Now, to some, February is viewed as the
shortest month of the year, and ever so often, we get an extra day
for this month… a day that we call a leap year; one extra day
gives the whole year a new name, but that's nothing deep. That's
just how we separate it from the other "28 day" February's. It's
amazing how one extra day can make the world of a difference,
literally. I digress. To a large portion of the world, February is the
shortest month, which also makes it the shortest wait for a pay
check, while others mark it as the month of love. To the rest of the
world, February is just another month…a month with a name. To
one family though, this month is special; God gave *Jewel.* Now, I
would like to think in a perfect world, when a new baby is
announced, a script would also be given; if so, it would go a little
like this: "It's a girl! She'll grow up fast in some areas; whereas,
in other areas, she may never grow properly. She will lose her
innocence at an early age and life will be seen in gray. Be gentle
with her, but not too easy because she may become insecure and
question your motives. The gray areas will make her question
things for a while, but don't place a label on her too soon because
one day, she'll grow into a woman; a woman misunderstood,
mishandled, mislead, and mysterious, but for now…she's a girl!"
Yes, in a perfect world, our lives would be attached to our births,
but that's not so in a world being perfected, such as we dwell.
Furthermore, such "announcements" would leave no room for
God's mercy and grace. Even if we could be warned of the "in
between phases" of our lives, we still wouldn't know what the end
would be. We may not choose our own worlds, but we do play the
leading roles in what shapes them. We take life one day at a time
because that's all we're given. If we controlled how many days
we could have, some of us would skip Monday's all together; the
irony in that is *still up in the air,* literally. We don't know if
Monday will bring rain or sunshine. Monday happens every

week, but the events of Monday, you will never see again. If you could control the days of the week, and you decided to take Mondays off of the table… what if God's plan was to bless you really big on the Monday that you skipped? Then, you would have MADE Tuesday to be…like what Monday is to you. What do I mean? Well, if you hate Mondays and God had a blessing for you "scheduled" for Monday, you will be miserable on Tuesday, waking up without that blessing. Would that be Tuesday's fault? See, the world turns, but what's in it for us? In some parts of the world, the sun shines while others see darkness. At some point, we all see day light. Winter stays a longer visit in Alaska, while the sun shines profusely over Yuma, Arizona; same sun, different shine. Every area of land needs the rain to bring the harvest, yield fruit, or cool and dry a thirsty land. Season's change and each change brings about its own personality and moodiness to say the least. Rain may fall from the sky for several days and we rejoice in this, knowing that that same sky will, someday, produce illuminating sunshine and we can, again, see our way…but where are we going? We love the sunshine, but we need the rain. The rain can feed, grow nurture and drown a thing all at the same time. This is how I feel about love. As for the rain though, we make the necessary adjustments, if we're prepared, or complain until the sun shines for us again.

Let's get back to abbreviations, though we're just talking about love. At times, abbreviations make our words incomplete. Now, to abbreviate is to shorten, reduce, cut, condense, or curtain. I make no attacks on abbreviations because some are good in their place. Have you ever tried to express a particular situation but could not find the right words to describe what you wanted to in ten words or less and you feel you're being too wordy but you're trying to "make" a point? Somehow, I feel as if I just gave you an example, without even trying to. Furthermore, more than likely, this is because there are some words and expressions that are too strong to be shortened, while at the same time, some words are strong enough to stand alone. Well, this is how I also feel about the word *love.*

We abbreviate the word love when we write, luv or luh; that's not so bad… at least it places "u" in the middle. The problem is, I can say, "I luv you" or "I luh you" and they would both sound the same, even though they are both a "short" form of love; no one would ever know the difference until I spell it out. Allow me to divulge this truth. A person may be superior in the connotation of the word love; however, this may have little to do with how they chose to explicate the action; the power is in the expression. See, if I said "I love you," I could still say, "Eye luv you" and it would sound like real love; no one would be concerned with the way I've said it... until I spell it out that way. Some would tell me that I spelled it out wrong, while others would choose to talk about it amongst themselves. I'm sure that some would accuse me of not knowing how to spell the word "I" or "*love.*" Why do we assume, when someone misspells a word, that they "should" know better? Who told you that I could spell out love? Is it because of my age or is it because of my look? When did you learn to love? How do you know it's the right way? How do you love? Have you ever had "the way you love" given back to you? How did it feel with you being on the receiving end? If it didn't feel good, does this make you want to "make" others feel the way you have been made to feel? Let's collect some more jewels.

Most Christians confess that Jesus Christ is the lover of their souls and I too share this testimony, though I've never heard Him say that He loved me. Don't be fooled; I can still see the writing on the wall. I can see His love for me when I look around and within. There would be no love from me without Him. I've found myself in places, in my life, that have caused me to become not so lovable, nor did I give my love easily. We say, "It's not what you say but what you do." However, it does matter what you say. We learn people by what they say; we judge people by what they do. Is that the same thing? Not necessarily. See, what you say reveals a lot about you; your actions just get you labeled. Let me give you a jewel: So, I could say, "I love children. Children are my life. I could baby-sit all day and night for free." Then, I could offer to baby-sit for you and then call you, at 1 a.m. to tell you to come and get your little munchkins because I can't take this babysitting thing anymore. Does this mean I am a liar? Not necessarily. What I said is how you learned of me; what I did reveals my heart. You could label me as a liar, but, if you looked closer, you could see that I may be a person who speaks "idol words; I say whatever I'm thinking and I don't think things all the way through before speaking. This could mean that I didn't pray about this decision, to watch your kids all night, before telling you I could...or, this could mean I LOVE children, but I am not graced to tolerate them. What you do is important...but that's because it's how we judge what you "say." It does matter what you say, but your actions can remove all doubt. If you say you love me, your actions towards me should testify to what you've said. If a person hears about the goodness of God and is still not persuaded, an encounter with God where He pulls them out, would make a believer out of them...if they recognize His hand.

26

Most of the time, that hand looks a lot like your neighbor's hand. Quite naturally, it matters what you say but if what you confess consistently doesn't add up, points are deducted from your "people" profile. Confession is good for the soul; furthermore, actions speak louder with more conviction. Much like faith works, confession without actions put a mute on one's words. If you "say it," a lot but you never "do it," the more you say it, the less people will pay attention to what you're saying. Speaking of mute, my voice has not always been the strongest in the room.

What's the easiest population to get lost in...large or small? Let me guess: "Large because the population is a crowd." This may very well be true but not in all cases. In small towns, life moves and people are identified by whose they are versus who they are. You're either Aunt Susie's girl, you're Uncle Avid's boy, you're cousin Itchie's wife or cousin twice removed. If you don't fit those descriptions, then... you look like Aunt Susie's girl, you look like Uncle Avid's boy, you look like cousin Itchie's wife or cousin twice removed. Everything and everyone seem to be connected and labeled despite their birth name, in small towns. Life moves by the process of association in small towns, so it doesn't matter to most who you are, what you do, or if you shine; just make the right connection and you'll be placed. Now, I make no attacks on small towns. I'm making a...connection. It's where I'm from and the word "small" here, is only used to paint a picture of the population size. Moving on, even if you don't quite make the cut, you'll still be labeled as the one that didn't fit, also known as the outcast. Now, I would love to tell you that I never fit in but that would be false; I never really tried. I labeled the labelers and stayed in my lane...if there ever was such a thing. If I could visibly see that I wouldn't fit, I didn't force it. How much can we trust our eyes anyway, though? We walk by faith and not by sight so what are the eyes used for? It is my belief that our eyes are used to....see. Our faith can cause our eyes to see whatever we believe. Faith alone is not enough. Faith's job is to *walk*...where you choose to walk has little to do with faith. It's up to us to use our other *sensors*. According to Acts 17:28, we live, move and exist through *Him*. So, why question your faith when things don't move the way they should? In order for things to flow, they must be done through Him (God). Why do we question Him when we chose not to walk through opened doors? It is obviously an issue of faith because we walk by faith. In the comfort of faith, we learn to run. I haven't always known about faith, but I have had my share of running.

I moved from one school to the next as a child. I told my mom that I missed my friends from each school, each time; I don't know if she ever really knew that the truth was that I felt rejected in both schools and felt my peers would accept me more if I gave them a little time to miss me. Where did this concept come from? In my child-like mind, I thought if people appeared to be frustrated with you or mistreated you, you needed to walk away and give them time to…invite you into their space. Hold on to that piece of jewel-ry; I'll explain where that concept came from, later.

I was a bit of a runner; when faced with life changing events, my first response was to erase it all and start over again. I eventually ran out of schools. Changing schools made me feel as though the past did not exist and I was free from it all. At times, though, I said to myself, "If freedom really feels like this, I would rather be bound." In one school, I was the teacher's kid, while in the other school, I was the weird "new" kid. I didn't like being weird, but a teacher's kid wasn't the easiest person to be; then again, I don't know anything about *easy*. At the new school, I was called the *new* girl; no pun intended, but I was far from *new*. The clothes and shoes that I wore were all hand me downs…you know, clothes that are passed down to you from someone else. At my previous school, this didn't matter because nobody really knew anyone from my hometown so I didn't run the risk of running into Betty Sue while wearing her old clothes, shoes or pants. However, at the new school, not only would I run into Betty Sue, I would also learn the truth about Betty Sue; I would find that I was not the new girl, but the "poor girl" that she gave all of her old things to. She couldn't resist bragging to everyone that I wore her old clothes, shoes and pants. I never really felt pressured to be someone that I was not, but I did feel the weight of those who thought I knew much more than I did. People know when you're insecure and it speaks louder than the loudest confidence. Your peers know when you're not confident; it gives off a scent. I don't know…maybe it smells life beef or something. See, people expect you to be who they think you are. Anything else requires too much thinking and you may not be worth their time. Our world consists of two groups: those who fit the mold and those that mold themselves to fit; anyone else is outside of the box and that's a peculiar person. It doesn't matter what organization(s), titles, or clicks you slide yourself into, if you don't fit the mold, you'll stick out in or over time. Though this is the road less traveled, the traffic of sight seers often crowd both lanes. Nevertheless, we ride, walk or run. Speaking of running, let's jog to the next chapter.

Love ink

     As a child, I didn't mind being, what some adults called, a doormat, though I didn't know such a thing existed. I knew that people used me more often than enough, but I couldn't prove it. The only thing I could prove was my own actions; I didn't speak up for myself and I knew some didn't mean me well, even if they treated me "well". I didn't like being used but...I hated rejection. My hate for rejection was far stronger than my dislike for being used. Being used often made me feel picked or selected; does this sound familiar to you yet? Before you start to *feel* yourself, let's collect some jewels. It takes patience and selflessness to deal with a situation that we chose. I am aware that some situations and things unravel before our very own eyes and I'm not talking about that.

     Let's get back to the doormat; it's funny how we interpret things to bring validity to our own actions and ways of thinking. One thing about a doormat though, is that a doormat always assumes that the norm is to be walked over and to feel heavy from the dirt and mud from other people's feet. There is a time and place reserved for us to cleanse ourselves and kick the dust from our own feet in a designated area. Doormats are made to lay down flat, low to the floor or ground, in front of most entrances and exits to serve their purpose. The problem comes when a stain glassed window decides (or is forced to) take on the role of a doormat...lying flat to the floor, sucking up all of the mud, dirt filth of other people's feet. Just because someone splashed a little dirt on you, that doesn't mean that, you now deem yourself a doormat. Even if you chose to "waddle" in the mud, that doesn't change who you are, but before you get up from the ground, let's explore how we sometimes get there. Travel with me, in your mind; even if you are still on the ground...don't waddle. We can imagine, most of us, what would happen if a stain glassed window decides to be a doormat; what could happen to the stain glass, eventually? Does it crack, stain or break? The window was originally made to reflect an image. As Christian, we believe that we were all created to reflect the image of God; how was He made, though?

Genesis 1:27 tells us that God created human beings in his own image, both male and female. No matter what we're covered with, we should still be made of what God is made of. He too knows about the *muddy* places of life. Hebrews 2: 9 tells us that God was given the task of becoming a little lower than the angels by suffering in death for us, although He is NOW crowned with glory and honor. It also tells us that the grace of God made all of this possible; now THAT'S what I call *amazing* grace. Hebrews also tells us, around the 14th verse, that God became like flesh and blood so that he could die and break the power of the devil. What is the devil's power? It's important to know such things in order to know the power that now is invested into us. Ephesians 2:2 tells us that the devil is a spirit which works in the hearts of people who refuse to obey God. If the word "obey" makes you feel a little uneasy, we don't even have to deal with that right now. Let's focus on the "heart". The devil works in the hearts of people. Does it say he works on the legs or twists' the arm of people? Let's move forward; we're still talking about love.

Growing up, I always struggled with my self-image or the lack there of; from my complexion to the size of my jeans, I just couldn't seem to fit; no pun intended...at least, not for me. Truthfully, I never wanted to fit. I just wanted everyone to let me be and for goodness sake, would somebody please tell me who I'm supposed to be! That's how I felt. Ever felt that way? Have you ever wished that "you" came with instructions and explanations? I couldn't quite put all of the pieces of me together; I couldn't collect *Jewel*. I experienced a lot of inner trauma as a child because I knew what I felt, but I didn't know why I felt it; moreover, I was not good with expressing my feelings in a healthy way. I didn't talk much, and if I did, it didn't come from the heart. I wrote poems and could release some things via pen, but I didn't know that, at the time. See, there's not much pain attached to being a doormat until you discover one day that you were not meant to be that way forever or, perhaps, you were never meant to be down as long as you were. I didn't know that writing was my gift of expression; I assumed it was the "thing" I was drawn to do, when I felt down. Nothing could bring my up quicker, than writing a poem or song. Now, I do have some great childhood memories; my family and I had some good times and made the best out of all bad times. I don't know how we processed those bad times, though. I remember being withdrawn from most people; I self-separated myself often. I always showed up on the scene consciously saying , "I already know that I'm different, so the least you can do is give me respect", but this is what I got the least of. Being teased was not an everyday thing for me, but when I was teased, I didn't handle that very well; I don't blame my peers much though. They didn't know what I went through on the inside. I was a depressed child who managed to hide it from the world...including those apart of my world.

31

They called me "sensitive;" that label stuck with me. I think it's easier to label someone as "the one who can't handle pain," than it is too admit that we may be habitual pain inflictors. People assumed that I was just the "the quiet girl." Though the teasing hurt at times, I was told by my mother that they were all jealous of what I had; now this was a hard pill to swallow, with or without water. I didn't feel as though I had anything that anyone would want. I saw myself as the most unfortunate person in the world: I was overweight, poor, never wore designer clothes unless someone else wore them out before me, I smiled a lot, talked a little, a bit of a push over and was still able to light up a room just by one smile or laugh, but that was no plus for me. My fear was that, once the room was "lit", everyone would see my imperfections and key in on them the way…I did. I never believed that my peers were jealous but I did know that they knew how I felt about myself. My mother used to tell me *the story* about how I got my name. As a child, I asked her to tell me *the story* often; I loved to hear it because it made me feel special. I didn't know what my name meant but *the story* made me feel its significance. I knew that I wasn't named *Jewel* by happen stance. She told me that one of her sisters wanted to give me a cute name that she'd created or discovered...can't remember exactly which one because that portion of *the story* didn't pull at me the most. She would tell me how she had gotten a revelation, just before I was born, to call me *Jewel*. I asked my mom to tell me this *story* over and over again because I knew there was something about my name…something that I didn't know. I knew I was missing some pieces to who I was, but I just couldn't seem to collect all of the pieces; I couldn't collect *Jewel*.

Love sick

She made it her business to call me *ugly* every day! I never really knew her name until she started making fun of me, daily. I only knew that she was popular, pretty to most, mean and had bad breath, obviously. Now, I don't know about the bad breath for sure, but I made that assumption by the constant frown that she made on her face. I didn't know why I was her focus. She didn't seem to have many friends, but she was well known, mostly by boys, and she was never alone. I could feel her presence when she entered the cafeteria without ever seeing her. She never said a thing to my face and for months, I had assumed that I had a complex; I thought that it was all in my head until one day, she put an end to my confusion. She shouted from behind me: "I can't stand her ugly pass!" Now, I added a "p" but "as" you can see, she didn't think much of me. Her "friends" laughed and sarcastically whispered to her, "Everybody likes her", and she responded, "Well, not me! She is so ugly to me!" I turned around, to my left side, in hopes that I was hearing my own voice; however, she attested my sanity by saying, "YES, YES, YES, I said it and I'm talking to YOU, Jewel!" I turned slowly and asked, "What did you call me?" She responded, "I called you ugly and you heard me!!" I said, "No, not that...did you call me *Jewel*?" She replied, "WHAT?!" She laughed and called me crazy. I said, "I'm just saying, how you' know my name and I don't know yours?" She assumed I was crazy; I assumed she didn't know I was being sarcastic; I had just called her a "nobody;" however, I felt the same. My friends told me not to worry about her and I went to my next class with a new title for myself: *Crazy Jewel*. Now, being called *ugly* didn't bother me as much as the fact that I didn't know who *Jewel* was. The bully thought it was weird for me to respond that way to my own name; I agreed. I took my name for granted often because I had assumed that it was just a name that people called me. They say, it doesn't matter what your name is, as much as it matters what name you answer to and that may be very true; however, if you don't have a clear understanding of the name that you were meant to be called, it doesn't matter how many times you answer. If you don't know who you are, you may still answer to your name or title without knowledge of its value. For example: Most children don't know that they're exposed improperly until they are exposed to something different from what they were taught. They assume that they are just like everyone else and everyone else is just like them, until the world shows them just how different they are. We know, as adults, that exposure is good in its place; out of place, exposure could be a curse. We learned this from what happened at that beginning of time: Why did Jesus really not want Adam and Eve to become aware of their nakedness? Did he really have plans for them to never become familiar with their own bodies? Had they already arrived to a place of an appreciation for their bodies? All throughout the bible, especially at the beginning, God created things in specific times and segments. We may not know exactly what Jesus' next step would have been, had Adam and Eve not gotten ahead of Him, but we do know that his plan for all mankind was to make him (mankind) in His own image. He too was exposed to the world at an appointed time. He came, He died, and He rose again with all of the power in His hands; perhaps, the power was in the obedience and process. Now, let's take a walk out of the clouds for a moment. Look at our own lives; what if we start a season too early or too late? Adam and Eve did. Oftentimes, our biggest mess ups, (if there is such a measure) are due to an out of date revelation. We show up at the party too early, but fail to bring our identification and we meet the bouncer at the door. It's like showing up for a swim class in a three piece suit; we look sharp, but we are not dressed for the occasion. It's not easy, at times to wait on God, wait for God or even wait with God and this is where we fall off of the horse. If that's not you, then maybe you can find yourself here: We show up for class late, without doing our homework and we expect and A for effort. We do things out of order and expect the world to sit still and ask us no questions. It's not always what we do but when we do it; I'm sure that you've heard that quoted a different way, but life has taught me the power of timing. If the timing is right, we won't have to worry about the "how you do it" quote. Good timing will take care of the "how to's" in any situation. How many times have we said, "If I knew then, what I know now, I would have handled that situation differently?" The truth, in most cases is, if we knew then what we know now, we would have never known that situation. Now, this next statement has to be read and understood with clarity, but I do tread softly, with my weapon in hand. IF truth be told, a lot of children are conceived out of time. We don't like to talk about or admit this because we, as human beings, have a hard time separating the *product* from the labor used to produce it. We find it hard to separate the person from the act or sin. We're not talking about sin…we are talking about people. Let's go back and look at two people in the bible: If Jesus didn't clothe Adam and Eve, the world, as we know it, may not be in existence. God saw the sin for what it was, but God saw His children for who He made them to be: they were made to produce more of Him. They were made in His image. When He covered the exposed bodies of Adam and Eve, He (God) was separating them from what they had done. As for you, your baby is still a precious gift from the giver of life; but the tools used to produce this product are still judged for whatever they may be.

Let's go back into the clouds for a minute. Now, Adam and Eve's disobedience went down in history and they were labeled as the two disobedient people who had everything and didn't value it; some even argue that only one of them was disobedient…but that's another story for another time. Their disobedience was still not strong enough to cripple their production; they were still able to produce greatness. What happened still didn't change what manifested in Genesis 3. I like to think that things fell into place at the point of exposure because they allowed God to cover them up. At times, we tend to try to cover our own selves up, not knowing that God has to do it because we don't really know what parts of us He intends to cover up. Jesus covered Adam and Eve exactly where He wanted them to be covered. He didn't cover their heads with shame, he didn't cover their feet to prevent further stumbling or their hands so they would never touch "disobedience" again; He covered their private parts… their secret parts. I'm sure there are times when our feet and heads need to be covered, but God knows those times. Eve named her first born *Cain* because she knew that God had caused her to bring forth life after all that she had done; Eve knew that this was a miracle. I believe she realized how God must have loved her. How would you have loved Eve? Can you blame God for covering her up? Would you have…cut off her hands for eating the apple? Eve honored God's mercifulness towards her. Much like Adam and Eve, we, at times, bite off more than we can chew; thanks to God's mercy and grace, we are still able to digest. We live to tell a story and we choose our attitude, but we can all rejoice in the fact that God judges no thing before it's time. There is a BIG gap in the process that leaves room for adjustments. No time is wasted time. The key is to move on with the right attitude, lest you become stuck in some ungodly cycle. I can tell you a lot about cycles but I'd rather you walk with me. Strap in, right here, because we may start to walk a little faster now.

It's o.k. if you can't forget the past; as long as you don't hold it hostage. Now, to forget is to fail to remember and to hold on is to cause to be or remain in one place, position or situation. Most people find it hard to separate the two, leaving themselves with the frustration of dealing with reality or the lack there of. We often wonder why life doesn't make sense, but we fail to consider the fact that life is not designed to make sense; life makes people and people make the *sense*. We are given life and whatever we make of it is what we call sense. If your life doesn't make sense, it's because some things are not quite adding up for you, but you are responsible for that equation. *Sense* is an awareness and appreciation for something. We are people, all over the world, trying to make life make sense and when it doesn't, it's not worth the living, we say.

At this particular point in my life, though, everything made too much sense. Ever been there? Have you ever been in a place, in your mind, where you thought you knew why everything turned out the way it did? As for me, I saw myself through the eyes of everyone and everything that had ever hurt me. My history and my mind tag teamed to confirm for me, all that I felt about myself. My mirror didn't look like God…it looked like *me*. I was convinced that my opinion of myself was the right opinion: I had a hidden weakness for math so I was "slow." I could make straight A's in everything other than math, so I was "lazy." I could write for hours and never have human contact, so I was "weird." I was overweight, so I was "fat." My father was not a part of my family, so I was "fatherless." I craved the attention of my father so I was "needy." My father was not around so I was "rejected." Little by little, I drifted away from people; they called me "shy" and I allowed them to give me that label. I was more comfortable with being called "shy," than I would have been, had they known I didn't like people. I began to keep my distance from people like never before; I did this because I knew that I wasn't the easiest person in the world to get close to. I was not comfortable with who I was and that's funny because I didn't quite know who I was. I was a virgin a lot longer than most of my peers unless they made up the same stories that I did. I didn't value my body so I made up stories, constantly to fit in; I would tell my peers how good sex was and how many times I'd tried it. The truth was that I would never give someone my body…I wasn't even comfortable with it. At times, I felt the world would be a better place without me in it. I started to see myself as…the person I painted myself to be: cheap. I didn't understand why God had made me the way He did…or the way I saw myself. I was sensitive, though very offensive, caring but not very trusting, giving, but I thought "you" were using me, smart but completely blind to the obvious, cheerful, but I cried a lot in private, understanding, though very much confused about me; to top it all off, I was friendly, but I didn't click well with most. I was…secretly battling depression and hiding it became a daily challenge for me. How do you love me? Who could love a person like that?

I remember hearing the saints telling me to hold on and hang in there because "even Jesus was rejected." That never made sense to me because I had nothing to hold on to other than my memories and my pain…furthermore, I didn't see myself as

Jesus. It's my belief that a person who struggles with the spirit of rejection must first learn who they are to totally be free from the person that they see in their mirror…then, such comparisons, like "Jesus" can be made. Furthermore, I was…selfish. See, rejection at times, comes laced with selfishness, causing a person to only see "them" in any situation. When I was told that "even Jesus was rejected," I couldn't see His rejection…I could only see the fact that He allowed ME to struggle alone. Jesus knew who He was, which made it easier for Him to hold on to his assignment; otherwise, coming down from the cross would have been a walk in the park with soft gel shoes. He held on to His assignment because He knew that it was an assignment and he knew the significance of why God chose Him to do it; He knew that He was the son of God, chosen for a cause. Don't get me wrong; I respected the wisdom of the saints and I know that most came from a pure place; they knew me far better than I knew myself and they assumed that I saw the same person they saw when they looked at me.

I never really had any direction but, I always seemed to end up in destined places; you know…places or positions that were obviously, strategically planned out for you, but you can't really explain how you ended up there. On the other hand, at times I felt God was with me…even when I was in a place where He didn't put me. These "destined places" often work for our good, but they are often places where God never intended for us to be, so He has to apply some grace for us to grow there.

Some places though, God allowed my other leader to put me there: my mom. She always wanted me to strive to be the best even if I was not the best at what I strived for. Mom knew that all of her children were skilled in the art of music so she pushed us harder to be a part of the arts offered at our school (s). My mom wanted me to be a part of the band. I started off being awesome, in the middle school band but once I made it to high school, I became the biggest joke in our high school band. Depression had secretly started to take over my life and nothing seemed interesting to me anymore. I had lost interest in the one thing that I cherished and loved the most: music. Most females in my high school band, stressed about putting that hard hat over their beautiful hair…while I secretly stressed about how I would make it back to the band hall by the time that I was supposed to be there; we did not own a car. I hated being late because it was just another reason for my band director to make fun of me. Giving someone gas money to pick me up was not an option because we had no money. My mother did the best she could for my brothers and me...worked two jobs and still couldn't make every end meet. It became the norm, to come home from school to a house with no lights. My peers didn't know that though...they assumed I was just late getting back to the band hall for game night. I don't know what my band director assumed but his actions and words showed me that he didn't think much of me; I remember stressing the most when we had away games because this would mean that we would stop for food and I would not have money to purchase anything. I don't know what hurt the most: starving or having to withstand that awkward moment of lying to my peers about my "sudden" stomach virus. I was either, sick, had already eaten or just didn't like the restaurant that we stopped at. This taught me to...lie.

In rank, I was always second band, last chair; if you don't follow, this means that I was the absolute worst performing player of our entire band in the trumpet section. I didn't rehearse my parts nor did I focus. Who had time for focus? I was poor, hungry and had other mature things to think about other than being a "child." I prayed a lot because this is what I was taught to do. My mother prayed for me and taught me the importance of prayer. I wasn't sure of how God loved me, but I was convinced that He heard my prayers. I knew God heard me but the spirit of rejection, that I harbored, led me to believe that God chose not to answer my prayers; I felt He rejected me. I believed God loved me...just as I believed my earthly father loved me, when he said it to me...whenever I saw him. Getting back to the band...

My band director made it easy for my peers to make fun of me because he did the same. I was an easy target. On a bad day, I would not crack a smile and surprisingly, most people knew to step off. On other days though, I laughed it off and cried later. I prayed a lot and held in my feelings. I hadn't learned, yet, to hear from God but my prayers sure eased the pain a little. I assumed prayer made me feel better because I could get those feelings out...somebody was listening to me. Because of my experience with my band director, I secretly labeled leaders as bullies and developed distrust for those in leadership. I thought leaders were people who were small enough to make fun of their followers, yet big enough for everyone else to follow their lead. I developed distrust for leaders who used their authority to make others feel small. After my senior year, I vowed not to ever play the trumpet again; I didn't know anything about vows though. I remained a part (or piece) of the band until I graduated from high school. I didn't get any better but I became the master of hiding my feelings from others. I went on to college…all guarded up and ready to…avoid the world. I wasn't sure if I could pull this off in college though.

Twisted Love

Surprisingly, I made it on to college; It was not easy, but life felt easier to manage; this was a good hiding place for me... not because of the freedom away from home, but because of the "new." I loved to start over. I loved "new" people because I could be...as closed up as I wanted to be. I never looked for ways to get away from home like most transitioning teenagers did; I just loved how people "love" you when they first meet you. People seemed to be crazy about you, until they see all of who you are. I didn't like that feeling. I loved to be the "new" person...quiet and shy, just the way people liked me. I loved comfort and acceptance. I went to college because I never wanted to be poor again and I wanted to be able to cover myself so that I would never have to depend on a man to do it. I secretly didn't trust men to keep their words; this motivated me to work so hard. I had seen my mom struggle alone, with broken promises, broken hopes, broken children and, most of the time...just broke. What I didn't see was her relationship with my father, who decided to leave us long before I was born. I listened to others blame my father for our hardships and pain so I developed a dis trust for men, financially. I believed that a man could love a woman but he would be more prone to walk out if the woman became pregnant with his children. I also felt as though my father didn't want me. I was often told that he left when the children came so my assumption, as a child, was that he wanted my mother but not me. I wasn't sure how he could love me. Let's get back to class though.

I stayed focused, for the most part, but my rejection issues, by this time, were in full effect. I never once went to the Thursday night parties and my peers assumed that it was because I was religious. I've always had a very strong sense of spiritual awareness, but that had nothing to do with the fact that I hated crowds. I didn't care to go to parties because of the crowd and I hated alcohol; I hated the very smell of it, though I'd never tasted it. I never tried alcohol because I didn't want to lose anymore of myself than I had already lost, and I didn't trust anyone else who was out of control of their own body. I didn't like any mind altering substance; my mind was pretty much already altered enough. Another thing that I loved about college was the fact that everybody was "the new girl". I didn't feel judged for being new, nobody knew where my clothes came from, nor did they care...and the ones who did care, were mature enough to whisper behind my back if they did have something to say. Nobody knew my story or where I came from, unless I chose to open up and share; I could manage my time, in college, to avoid the whole world, if I wanted to. If I didn't want to socialize, I could walk to class early and already be seated when others came in. If I didn't want to see anyone that day, I could stay in my room. If I wanted to study in private, there was always that little space on the second floor of the library where no one would even know that I was there. The college life helped me to…protect my depression. We have a tendency to protect our dysfunction(s), although we tell ourselves we're hiding them. Subconsciously, we don't want anyone to…bother our dysfunctions. We defend our dysfunctions and vouch for them. Instead of apologizing to those offended by our dysfunctions, selfishness causes us to…further explain the reason we "are" the way we "are." As for me, there were times that I wanted to come out of my shell. The thing about being in a shell is, the shell protects us from the outside world but traps us inside of the world we've created. Furthermore, anyone who runs into that shell could get hurt by it.

My college experiences helped me to deal with my communication insecurities. Before undergrad, I wasn't comfortable with public speaking or speaking out at all. I was no social butterfly but in college, I learned to do what I had to do…even if I had to speak out. I had one professor, in particular, who pushed me to come out more; I never knew what made him believe there was more to me than I displayed. He made me the president of the social work association on campus. I tried my best to fail as best as I could, just so they would crown someone else with that crown of thorns. I didn't want the responsibility of having to rely on myself for information, communicating that information to my peers or…well, let me just be open: I didn't want to be a leader. I didn't know much about leadership but it was my belief that a leader was (is) someone who has to show up early, leave late, stand in the gap for those who don't do their jobs, communicate effectively and be very understanding. To me, this seemed like a lot of personality that I didn't feel I possessed. Leaders couldn't…blame someone else for decisions made.

I don't know if I really learned to trust God in my young adult years, but I sure trusted someone other than myself. I was broke most of the time and never really focused enough to study anything that didn't interest me. I was still poor, unsure, uncommitted, and inconsistent; these were the qualities that I was most known for. I didn't want to commit to things or people because, I feared things would change and that would ultimately cause me to get hurt. Everything was about me. I rejected things because I didn't want to be…rejected. I rejected people because I wanted to reject them before they rejected me. The twisted part of this is, I didn't think about how I could have made others feel.

I had little self-esteem, and I still struggled with the spirit of rejection throughout most of my young adult life. The older I got, the more I could control the illness on its own terms; what I mean by that is, I was able to conceal my emotions and feelings unless I wanted to be open. I could control my crying spells, appear to be comfortable when I wasn't and appear to be strong…when I wasn't. It's the same way that most alcoholics are unable to control their ability to give in to alcohol, yet they are in control enough to stay away from "Big Momma" at the family reunion because they just CAN'T allow her to see them that way. We claim we can't control certain actions, but we seem to be able to control who, when and where we display those actions. I still internalized everything, but I didn't always show it. I would allow different people to reach out to me from time to time, but if I felt, for one minute, that they didn't understand me, I would shy away or become offensive, verbally or non-verbally: non-verbally if you left me alone; verbally if you cornered me for a response. I was more confrontational in college than I was in grade school but I didn't know why; maybe the free will of expression got to me. I still didn't bond well, though I met some really cool people, who we'll call friends. I quickly found my place in the school choir and found comfort in singing as I had done so before; I didn't like being the center of focus though. They discovered I could sing lead and pushed me to lead several songs. This only…pushed me away because I was secretly intimidated by those I felt sang better than I did. I wanted to go ahead and…fail so they would stop depending on me to show up for rehearsal. The choir assumed that someone had hurt me and wanted to know if there was something they could do to fix it; they wanted answers…so did I. The truth is, they had no idea how deep that question was; furthermore, my "pain" had nothing to do with them…and "fixing me" was something they didn't even want to try and tackle. I wouldn't wish that on my worst enemy.

I heard there was a band! I knew that I possessed the skills to play the trumpet, but my flashbacks from high school haunted and taunted me. One of my associates talked about joining the band and someone told the band director that I was a trumpet player; he sent for me. He told me that I could get a scholarship for joining the band so I gave it a shot. I know what you're thinking; I know I previously vowed to never pick up a trumpet again. Well, the thought of extra money for school was my motivation. I never intended to do my best in the band, but I wanted to be able to support myself in school so I did join. I told myself, "It doesn't matter if you get last chair…as long as you're in the band, you can get paid for it." I just knew that I would get last chair. I didn't apply myself much because I wasn't in it to win it and it showed in my attitude. Surprisingly, my ability to play the trumpet was not the issue; my attitude was. I was quite rebellious and sweet all at the same time. This made it very hard for the director to confront me about my rebellion. I wasn't mean or snappy; in fact, I didn't say much. I just…didn't do what I was asked to do, at times. The director was patient with me, though I showed up late, didn't bother to show up at all, tried my best if I liked the song we were playing, and dared him to correct me about any of it. I didn't verbally dare him; I just…didn't heed to his warning and my peers took notice. At times, I came across as cocky, but the truth was that I didn't believe in myself and I didn't believe anyone who believed in me. My college band director was automatically a "liar" by default; why? Because he told me something different than I'd heard in the past; he told me that I was a great trumpet player. How could that be true? Somebody had lied to me; either my high school band director or my college professor of band. The truth was, my high school band director had…never told me that I was the worst. My performance placed me in last chair, second band. How could you love a person like me? The truth was that I had been stripped of all confidence, in that particular area, so the whole thing seemed like a big joke to me. I loved music; I just held on to my past. I expected my band director to love me the same way that my high school band director did. I knew that my ways were confusing and quite frustrating for my college band director, but I often wondered how he tolerated me. How did he love me? How do you love a person like me?

Obviously, college is different form grade school, but my whole experience was different. I still struggled with who I was in college, but I didn't deal with resentment. I loved the school of my choice and I grew to love most of the people there. I can't really name one person, all four years added together, that I just didn't like. Even the most irritating person seemed like family. People still judged me, but for the most part, they judged me from a pure place. I was *Jewel.* When I smiled all of the time, I was named Smiley. If I chose not to speak, I was called shy; when I chose to open up, I wasn't called weird or clingy…I was called friend. I loved the college life and like most, I hid out there for at least four years. I did learn that the whole world didn't love me the same way. I started to finally look at the way I loved…me.

During my college years, I discovered a way to clear my head; my understanding of it though, was still foggy. I discovered that I liked the company of men; I'd never really liked it before. What I saw, in college, was…men didn't talk as much as women. I wasn't comfortable with people who talked too much. I fell for an African guy who treated me like a queen, behind closed doors. Now, I didn't fall in love; I just fell. We never dated but I could call him when I felt down or rejected by the world. This was every, other day. He used me when his studies were getting the best of him and I used him when the world had gotten the best of me; this was… every, other day. After missing a cycle one month, I called him to inform him that I could possibly be pregnant. He told me, "Good luck and I hope you find the father!" I didn't believe in luck…but I sure did believe I needed to *find the Father* but not the same father that he was speaking of. This is the point in my life when I knew that something was missing. I started to really see my resentment towards not having a father of my own, in my life and not being raised by my father. I started to realize how angry I was. Yes…at this point, I needed to find the *Father*.

I reached out to my earthly father several times during college and he tried to make things better, but it was far too late. My trust for him was nonexistent and I felt he owed me something, but I didn't know how much or what he owed me, for that matter. I didn't know him well enough to blame him, yet I knew enough about me to know that…he could possibly be the blame. I started to really see the voids that I had but I really didn't know how to fill them or what to fill them with. The pregnancy scare turned out to be a false alarm; the African guy told me that he assumed I was sleeping with someone else because, he and I had never really had sex. I didn't know much about sex; apparently, neither did he. He told me that he could never "get in" so he didn't force it. I assumed he was talking about my heart…he assumed, he was talking about my body. He apologized but I tucked that apology away, in my heart and said I would decide, later, if I wanted to accept; I never bothered to put his name on it, so it got mixed up with the rest of the things in my heart. After that day, I vowed to never have "none sex" again. I didn't know much about vows though. As crazy as it seems, we're still talking about love.

Conditional Love

Sometimes, it's easy to assume that we've grown up because of the stripes that we wear. We often assume that we've grown from a situation or thing just because we made it through it…or did we? Did we grow, or did life just…keep moving? There is a difference between growing wiser and just growing up. Life moves on whether we grow or not; life's only purpose is to come and go; how we live life is up to us. We can choose to grow from life's mishaps or we can wait it out: Wait for life to pass us by. This is why life happens to us again and again. The cycle of life moves with the wind, and before long, you'll be faced with a similar situation again; the choice you make is up to you. I've heard it said before that only a fool uses the same numbers twice and expects a different outcome. While that statement may have some point of validity, its best, at times to make sure you've tried adding the same numbers you have, subtracting the numbers, multiplying and even dividing before throwing the numbers out altogether. Sometimes, it's not the numbers but it's the method. Starting over is not always such a good thing; it may even work, but was it your best decision? It makes us feel big to start over because we don't have to face anything from our past that might have caused us pain…or we may not even know what to do with pieces we have left. This is what we fear; we are afraid that if we use the same "numbers," we won't be able to get past the thought of, "THESE numbers didn't work for me before so why should they work now?" Let's bring it closer to home: if you fail at an attempt to open up your own cookie shop, does this mean, "People aren't buying cookies so I need to open up a cake shop." Maybe it's not the cookie…it's the method you used to open the cookie shop. Maybe it's the way you treat people when they enter your doors of your business. It's unwise to start over without knowing what worked before. Even if you know what didn't work, find out what did work and don't throw "those numbers" away. If you had a failed marriage but you were a good cook, keep "cooking;" don't vow to never cook for a man/woman again, just because the relationship failed. We do this; when something fails, we take what DID work and vow to not waste our time giving the best of us again. Keep using what did work; look closely at what did not work. You may have been a good cook but…how was your attitude?

We can start over but a new heart is what we need. See, we can change all of the numbers in our lives…we can move away to another city or we can choose to avoid the whole world, but our hearts will still remain with us; we could ultimately, get the same results if we don't change our hearts (the way we judge, see and process things). We're still talking about love.

Maybe the saying "love is what love does" needs clarity. We must first learn the characteristics of love before we accuse love falsely. If love is what love does…does anybody know what love is… supposed to do? Proverbs 10:12 tells us that love covers over all wrongs, while Zephaniah 3:17 suggest that God can use His love to quiet us; then, John 14: 15, tells us that love compels us to obey God. If we look at Romans 13:10, we learn that love keeps us from harming our neighbors…just to mention a few characteristics of love. Love is also described in I Corinthians 13; it says that love is patient, kind and is not happy in evil. It says that love never fails. So, love covers, love makes a person want to obey God (no matter how He shows up), love does not harm (even if it wants to), love is willing to wait, and love always wins.

A thing called love

By my college graduation time, I had assumed that I knew how to love; I thought I knew what love looked like. I thought love was a feeling and if I didn't have a "feeling," that wasn't love. I knew how to love, but not past my "feelings." I moved to another state, although I wasn't clear about why I had to move there. I assumed it was because my town was small and going back home could have meant wasted time looking for a job. I chalked it up to one of my *destined places* journeys. In this place, I fell for another man; I didn't fall in love…I just fell. I fell for his interest in who I was. I had dated guys before, but he was quite different. He had a genuine interest for who I was, what had made me the way I was and all that he thought he knew about me. When I met him, I was lonely. I didn't have many friends because I was in unfamiliar territory and I didn't trust those around me just yet; the irony in this is, I entered a relationship with him, without even knowing who he was. I was selfish. He needed me and I needed him. We were both…needy. The irony in this is, I needed him and I…needed him to need me. He was ill, physically and I was ill mentally. He came to the table with his illness; I *ate* but pretended to digest. When it was my turn to "talk," I told him my mouth was full. Some things go down easy until we discover, later, what ingredients were used to make that particular thing. A person may show you a scar that they were born with, but it's up to you to continue to search for other scars they don't show and to explore the making of that one scar. They might tell you, "This scar comes from a time when I burned myself in the kitchen." What they may not tell you is, "This scar comes from a time when I burned myself in the kitchen, trying to get away from my abusive step-father." When they fail to inform you about the origin of that scar, hidden scars may "pop" up later that you didn't see before. That "emotional scar" that step-father left on them, could be damaging to your life, that you are trying to spend with them. On top of that, they may still have some other scars, illnesses or habits that they created alone; those are the ones that you need to see. The other scars, you need to know.

Even though I didn't show this particular man all of my past scars, he thought he knew the explanation for the scars he could visibly see on me. I was shy so that meant I had "low self-esteem." I was overweight so that meant I had "low self-esteem." I cried a lot, so that meant I was "sensitive...and had low self-esteem." Sometimes, we see the obvious but we don't investigate what the obvious means for us, if we choose this person. For example, if you are over-weight and your husband/wife calls you "fat" when he/she is angry with you, it might make you feel down; however, what if your husband/wife calls you fat and someone else calls you *thick and sexy?* How will you respond to that "someone's" interpretation of the "thing" that your husband/wife identified as a negative? What if someone, outside of your marriage "renames" something, with a compliment, that your wife/husband names negatively? How would you respond? If you don't already see yourself in a positive light, scars and all, you might take that "new" name to heart and assume the "outsider" sees something that your husband/wife doesn't see; you are right…but you have the wrong idea. The outsider does see something: an opened, uncovered space. The outsider is not looking for your "heart;" he/she is looking for…an opened, uncovered space to squeeze into your marriage. If you respond inappropriately, what does this mean for you? Are you justified just because your husband/wife doesn't appreciate who you are? Do you…know who you are? How do you love you? If you respond inappropriately, you have now taken on another title for yourself: wrong and scarred. When we are "scarred and wrong," it's not very easy to get the healing that WE need; Why? We assume somebody owes us an apology, but we offend so many others along the way…leaving God no choice but to deal with our offense first. What does this mean? Example: if a teenage child gets angry because he's tired of being beaten by his mother every night, and decides to take a loaded gun and shoot up his school, the "law" would be called to the crime scene long before the psychiatrist or lawyer is called in. As a matter of fact, getting the "loaded gun" out of the child's hand, would be the first priority. This is how God deals with us when we are "scarred and wrong;" If you have a tendency to attack and shoot people with your words, when you are down and depressed, God will deal with your tongue, the loaded weapon, before dealing with your broken heart, that may be the cause of your angry outbursts. The way we respond to our circumstances, moves us from being the victim to the offender. Now, if God is going to do any healing, He may have to deal with your "wrong" first. Relax! We're still talking about *love.*

I didn't trust a soul, by the time that I was married… including the person that I married...but he was easy to talk to. I know what you're thinking: "Did I skip the part in the book where she tells us she married the man she "fell" for?" See that's the point…I didn't tell anyone I was marrying him; we just…went to the courthouse and said some vows. We had both admitted to one another that the physical attraction was not there, at the beginning, but we developed a love for each other along the way. We didn't date long because I feared jumping in the sheets with him. Not to mention, he called me "family" and that meant a lot to me at this time. When I met him, I was just at the break of becoming officially sick of myself; however, God had just started to…tell me that He had chosen me to preach the word of God. Really? Now? I heard Him clearly; I just…heard too much of *me* as well. I had started to really see myself for who I was…not for who I was intended to be. I didn't like what I saw, so I panicked. I was afraid that I had officially lost my mind; I made this assumption because, I didn't see how God could love me… much less choose me to be a voice for Him. I didn't feel chosen and I didn't know what it was to be chosen or picked. I felt rejected by everyone and everything around me. I wanted to get married and become somebody's something. Both of my brothers had gotten married and had started their own families and I felt…misplaced, replaced and all over the place. I feared being alone…but I felt alone. What a confused person I was; however, I was clear about one thing…I didn't know how anyone could love a person like me.

He was in transition, so he didn't have a place of his own; I opened my home to him. They say home is where the heart is; I didn't know about that. As for him, I don't know his motives and it's not my place to tell you that he used me…especially since I…could have been accused of doing the same. I was settled with being single, when I met him but I didn't like being "alone;" it made me feel rejected. I was just starting to see bits and pieces of *Jewel,* but I should have waited for all of the pieces to come together. Instead, I gave him "pieces of me." In the past, I had magnified my flaws but I didn't magnify my faults: this is the deception of internalized rejection. Low self-esteem and rejection work hand and hand to deceive a person into believing that they were dealt a bad hand; it tells you that you're ugly, you're too black or too white, you're too small or too fat, you're too slow or too fast; however, never once does it bring to the surface those qualities about you that may be…not so delectable. When we look at our faults, we may find that…we may NOT be too fat, but we do need to learn some self-control when it comes to eating food. Maybe we're not too slow but we do need to learn how to move with a sense of urgency. If we magnify our flaws (outward appearance), we will never take the time to take a look at those things that may not be good and need to be changed…like our attitudes, our love walk or the lack thereof; what about looking at our hearts? We don't want to do that. Those are the things that matter the most and can open or shut a door right in our face. Those bad thoughts can cause a person to become selfish and it's harder to see because the person feels as if the problem is something beyond their control, like their appearance, shape or speech...craftiness at BEST!! Sometimes, we just need someone to tell us, "Hey, you are not ugly but your attitude is!!" The enemy would never want us to actually work on our faults; he would rather us obsess over our flaws. Why? Our flaws (outward appearance) are GOD's doing. Our inward appearance (the heart) is what WE'VE exposed ourselves to. The enemy's fight is against God; he wants to make God's work look bad. Faults are simply errors; it doesn't matter how they happen, they can always be corrected, changed or explained. A flaw is much similar to a fault and this is where we're deceived; a flaw is more of a blemish or imperfection. I don't know if I've ever seen a perfect person, without seeing a liar at the same time, but I haven't been all around the world. Needless to say, if I had seen one, I would have missed it because I don't know what *perfect* looks like.

I obsessed over my flaws and having to see my faults made me weak. I started to realize how selfish I had become and how I victimized myself. I had never been forced to deal with the "whys" of me before meeting the man I married. Something about marriage tends to reveal your true self. As for me, all of my "whys" in the past started with F's: I had blamed my father's absence for all of my troubles. I knew that I didn't like for people to leave my home without saying goodbye, but I didn't know why I didn't like it. Throughout the course of my marriage, the man I married would point out my flaws and faults to me...I didn't care to hear either. I didn't trust his judgment because my flaws were no longer my own insecurities but they were now his as well. I was open with my husband but I didn't share everything. This became frustrating for him because he knew that he didn't know everything about me. He knew that he had married someone that he didn't know and we both knew that we had made a mistake, but tried to fix it by showing the world, that we could make it work. We made the world our enemy; "me against the world" became our theme song, but did we make sweet harmony?

I didn't tell whole truths; the other "half" of that story is...I was a liar. No pun intended. I only told my husband bits and pieces of me; he labeled this as deception...I labeled it as "I didn't know all of the pieces of me". Everything I learned about me, during the course of my marriage, was not bad. I learned a lot about my spiritual gifting. I had always been a vivid dreamer and so was my husband. I never realized just how prophetic my dreams were until I got married; I didn't consider myself as being prophetic. I knew that I could feel the emotions of others very easily and could dream about people every other night, but I never took the time to share any of my dreams or interpret, in the past. I was often amazed at my husband's ability to dream about things that I had never shared with him; I didn't know that I was doing the same and for a while, he didn't tell me. I would share things with him and although his expression said, "how did she know that", his mouth would say, "what are you talking about?" I shared my dreams with him and at times, those dreams would come to pass. I could dream about someone betraying me and soon after, that dream would come to pass. We were both dreamers and sharing our dreams were the highlight of our marriage, at times. Other times, it just caused confusion. How could dreaming cause confusion? Well, let's consider this: If you have a group of people who can see the "way" yet, none of those people have legs to walk, they still won't get far; the most they can do is sit around…in one spot…and share all that they see. Our marriage was not enjoyable because we often spent time discussing everyone who was not there for us, how we were not there for each other, our faults, our flaws and everything else that seemed to be going wrong. We would have these times that we'll call *confession times.* These were the times when we would tell each other how we felt about our lives together so far. We had been married for a couple of years and the fighting never stopped. We fought the world, we fought each other, we fought our families, we fought each other, we fought ourselves, and then we started all over again fighting the person closest to us. In spite of it all, every fight and every disagreement brought me closer to who I was…there were times, though that I wished my mirror would have stayed foggy. I didn't like who I saw.

      I decided to quit my job to force my husband to work; little did I know, this would make things worse for us. I'm not saying that he wouldn't work…I'm saying that I quit my job to make him work. We were not prepared for this because I provided the largest portion of our income; I was also in school at the time and had gotten extremely stressed out. I took another job; I was asked to quit my next job because I had started to develop manly characteristics and stayed up all night trying to figure out how my family would make it financially. He assumed I had just developed these manly qualities…I assumed he didn't pay attention enough. Never the less, he was right in asking me to take a break from work, but our funds didn't add up enough for me to do so. He would wake up to find me in the living room crying and praying to God, in my heavenly language, but my actions were beginning to show that I thought I was in hell. I could pray and cry out to God for hours, in my heavenly language, and get up from the floor with bags underneath my eyes. I could stay up all night and sleep for an hour the next day while he went to work, when he found another job. I stopped caring how I dressed when I went out because it just...didn't matter anymore. My life consisted of praying, crying and hiding depression from the world around me. At times, my husband would express what he and his family felt about me and their first impression(s) of me. Even when he apologized, later, for the way he told me, I still tucked the pain away in my heart, along with every other pain I had tucked there. I had planned to go back later and decide if I wanted to forgive them; once again, I didn't put a label on that "pain" so, somehow, it all got mixed in...together...with everything...and everyone else in my heart that had ever hurt me. I didn't leave my marriage, at this time though, even though we had both expressed how we felt about one another.

A financial crisis, or should I say the lack of finances finally got the best of us, and we moved to Florida with my husband's family. I knew things would change, drastically because I knew that I had not grown to trust them yet...or him yet...or...I just didn't trust. Never the less, I was determined to stand by my husband's side...however, somehow, I ended up standing on his front and the whole world was standing on top of us. Besides, I had scared everyone else away. I made it...hard for others to love me. I had played around with offense and had gotten stuck in it; my feet were planted and it wasn't easy to break free from this sticky mess under my feet.

I packed my little things and prepared to move. I kept a secret suit case though; in this suit case, I kept all of the pain that I felt he had caused me as well as all of the hurt and shame that I had ever experienced my whole life...I didn't bother to put any labels on which "pain" was caused by him so, somehow, everything got "mixed" together in my heart...along with everything and everyone that had ever caused me pain. This wasn't very fair to him, but it sure gave me a place to dump off everything, once we made it to our destination. I blamed him for everything that had ever happened to me. My husband became a *human target* for my pain; he was an easy target and I could easily throw any dart and hit the bulls-eye. I didn't know how he loved me, but it sure felt familiar to me; his love felt like *rejection*. I assumed love was a feeling…and rejection is how I felt.

Once we were moved, things got out of hand very quickly and neither of us could pull the pieces back together. My husband's health was seemingly getting worst and I was the only person who was able to work. We both became more depressed and couldn't help each other. I hated the very thought of divorce and split families; though a part of me knew that this marriage wouldn't last, I wanted to keep my family together…he was my family. We found ourselves doing the one thing that we had done our whole marriage, thus far: we defended our marriage. Even if we argued in private, we were very protective of one another and wouldn't allow others to disrespect one of us. My husband became very ill and I woke up one morning to find him watching one of his favorite movies that we had watched several times throughout the marriage. We had grown apart, physically, as bitterness had started to take root and grow thorns. My bitter roots produced anger; I had never been a person to express anger before, so this monster felt different growing inside of me. I'm not sure of what bitter roots produced in him, but I do know that we both changed and began to treat each other the way we secretly felt about ourselves. Day by day, I was beginning to pour out and express my disappointment, embarrassment and discomfort to my husband, but I never got a chance to TELL him. You read it right; I expressed my anger but I didn't do it verbally. My silent actions spoke much louder than his loud voice. One day after we had just watched our favorite movie, *Pursuit of Happyness*, my husband felt the need to open up to me. He apologized to me for the awful turn that our marriage had taken; he apologized for how our lives had changed, for the worst, since I'd met him; he assumed that this was the worst I'd ever seen. I don't know if he was right or wrong in his assumption, but I did know that pain was no stranger to me. He told me that his body was starting to show signs of getting worst; he had a physical illness. Right in the middle of his sentence, he began to twitch and his mouth began to twist; he was having, what some doctors call, a grandma seizure. Now, before this time, I had my share of tucking things away in my heart, but those things were usually things that offended me; this was different though because my husband was ill. Never the less, I had no time to…put a label on this one so…somehow…it got placed into my heart…along with everything else that had ever caused me pain. I had planned to go back, process things and put a label on this one that read, "Not his fault," but…I didn't get around to making a label for this one so…in my heart, it went along with everything else. Now, I was no stranger to tucking things away, but I always did it for me. I put away my feelings and the fact that I was planning to leave him; I never told him, that day, that I had contacted my family to send me money to leave. All of his family came into the room to care for him and call the ambulance; I left the room after his family entered the room to call the Lord. I had learned to pray and this became the norm for me. I prayed for my husband and he didn't die that day. I don't know if he lived because of my prayers, but I knew that I needed to pray that day. My husband was hospitalized for several weeks, but the hospital was an hour away from where we lived…no pun intended; I had to spend nights at the hospital, by his side, watching and waiting for him to come back to himself. I had no money, no gas in the tank, and I nearly starved every day. I decide to take on a job at a fast food restaurant, after my husband was hospitalized for an extended time, but that was a disaster. I would go to work, come back to the hospital, eat a little food from his tray and then pray that God would make a way for us. I didn't starve because I had nobody in my life to help me; I starved because I'd built a bridge between myself and those who loved me; this bridge was burned once I crossed over it. I knew that my mind was slipping though. I didn't look the same. My self-image was never ever really the best, but now, I didn't even obsess over my flaws…I just didn't bother to look at myself altogether. Sometimes in life, we are forced to put our feelings to the side as life demands our attention to an area where someone else's situation calls for our full attention. Although I chose to be the "good wife", that bitter monster grew inside of me and increased daily as I fed it a bunch of….bull. I told myself that things would never change and that I had gotten myself in this mess and only death would free me from it. I told myself that God couldn't love a person like me because everyone who I thought loved me had turned their nose up or their backs over. I told myself that I could not be any more rejected than I already was. After I told myself all of these things…I remembered that I was…a liar. Truth be told, I believed that God loved me…and I believed that my natural father loved me…and I believed that my husband loved me…and I believed that my family loved me…the same. I wasn't sure of HOW they all loved me.

In the midst of all of the dead situations around us, we managed to create a life; I became pregnant. We were both pretty shocked and excited about the baby to come although we knew our relationship had taken a big blow. We rushed to the clinic just days after finding out, only to be informed that we had some complications in pregnancy. I didn't know much about pregnancy and had no idea that special attention was needed...I didn't know that I was pregnant. I didn't have a doctor yet, so I had no primary care physician to follow up with. I was depressed beyond measure and felt as though the heavens were frowning on me. I frowned back, but I didn't look towards heaven: I looked at my husband. A few weeks later, I started my cycle...at least that's what I thought. I woke my husband up one night with violent pains in my lower abdomen. Before then, I laid there in pain for several hours without waking my husband up because I assumed that I was having a bad monthly. When the pains started to come stronger and I could actually time them, I knew that something was wrong. I woke my husband up to inform him that something was wrong. I screamed quietly...this was common for *Jewel* to do; I had done so, most of my life. We rushed to the hospital; I was sure that I was going to die that night and had told my husband that I loved him and I was sorry for everything. The doctors never checked me out; they sent me home with some pain medication, assuming that I was having a bad monthly. The medication took the edge off so I was able to get some sleep, but the pain was still there. The next morning, the pain went away after I miscarried. I called my husband to the bathroom so that he could see what I had passed. This only added to my bitterness because I felt as though God had taken something from me, but I didn't blame Him for it. I knew that I didn't deserve such a gift...a gift of life. I wanted to blame God, but I was too religious for that. I wanted to blame my husband but he was ill and didn't need the pressure. I only had one other person to blame: myself. I didn't know who to trust or who to talk to, so for a while, I chose to keep silent. So...I placed this pain, into my heart, along with everything...and everyone else that had ever hurt me; this time, the pain was too unbearable to deal with so...I didn't put a label on it. I just tucked it away in my heart and somehow, it got mixed together with everything and everyone else that had ever caused me pain. I could feel the bitter monster growing more and more inside of me. I didn't want to love anymore and I questioned everyone who had ever said they loved me. I assumed love was a feeling and I wasn't feeling it anymore, yet...I wanted everyone to love me. How could they? How do you love a person like me?

Despite the hell, I had learned to trust God on a different level now; nothing deep about it. I just knew that someone, other than myself, was keeping me alive. However, the bitter taste in my mouth began to seep out through my breath. Most hurt heals over time, but what about harm? Harm is physical or moral injury. Violent winds are acts of nature, yet they can destroy everything in their paths. Maybe this will sound familiar to some of you: "I don't mean any harm, but…" We love to say that "but" takes away everything a person has said prior to the "but", but that's not always true. The "but" adds another twist or wind to the person's previous statement…it can add or take away; any way the wind blows. So then, the "but" can twist and the mouth…well, the mouth turns. Words are so amazing because it only takes one word to change a lifelong situation. At times though, we can't find the right words to say, so we settle for "it is what it is".

Preying... for love

Everything about me, at this point in my life, was bitter. I didn't smile anymore, I had no motivation, and love was the last thing on my mind, yet... the first thing I talked about. How was that so? I felt undeserving of love but I desired to feel it so much; I wanted to feel what people talked about, concerning love, but I wouldn't dare admit it. At this point in my life, I stopped *praying* and began to *prey*. It's easy to confuse the two: praying is our communication and conversation with God. Preying is when we complain to God about everyone around us, asking him to get them and make us out to be victorious; this is still a form of communication but our motive makes the difference. When we prey, we look for what we feel we need to sustain us; we don't want answers...we want revenge and justification. I still talked to God... morning, noon and night, but our conversations were one sided; I did most of the talking because I complained, nagged and then told Him (GOD) that I understood if He was mad at me and didn't want anything to do with me. I bluffed God; I told Him that I would just keep silent because He wasn't listening to me anyway. I knew this wasn't true...it just made me feel better; this way, if I felt He didn't hear me, I wouldn't have to feel rejected because I said it first...right? I dealt with God the same way I dealt with people. I had always separated myself first so that no one could reject me any more than they had already done. I had assumed that God teased me the way so many others had because some of the people who had hurt me were indeed His people. I looked for any reason to disconnect from people and I preyed on those who had hurt me. I would reach out to them constantly, in hopes that they would NOT reach back so that I could tell God about it. I monitored the people I had once looked up to...especially God's people. I watched their reactions to my situation(s)...only to find that you often get just what you give out. I couldn't blame any of them because I knew that I was not easy to love. I found it hard to love me, so I could image how others loved me...then again, I couldn't.

I made an effort every night to pray and I never stopped praying. Even if my day was filled with what I knew as hell, I still found a way to pray. Some nights, those prayers were weak and would even start off by calling the name of "Jesus" several times and then falling asleep. I learned the bible like never before because I consistently searched for God in it. Now, some people read the bible for many different reasons and I too have gone through many different changes with my motives for searching the word…but in it, I found the word; It never changes, no matter what your motives are. I once read the bible out of routine; I read it every morning just because it was the "thing to do…you know? "A scripture a day keeps the devil away!" Yeah right!! I quickly discovered that wasn't true. During my season of bitterness, I searched the bible. This season lasted a long time. I wanted to see what God had to say about everything that I was going through. I wanted to see what caused bitterness, what caused hate, what caused anger and if anyone in the bible had ever been through any of those things and came out victorious. I began to tell my husband that the bible said, "The way of a transgressor is hard." We both constantly complained that everything seemed so hard for us and nothing came easy. I loved the book of Proverbs because it taught wisdom and I didn't feel wise. Proverbs 13:15 was the scripture that I labeled myself with. The first thing that became clear to me, as I read the word, was that… I was not clear about anything. I had no clear understanding of what I was going through or the decisions that I had made. It is my belief, that at any point in a person's life, they should be able to find themselves in the bible. At times in my life, I felt like Job while other times, I felt like the blessing of Abraham. At this particular time though, I felt like Cain: un-Abel...pun intended. I felt God rejected me and I didn't know why. I wasn't sure of how He loved me.

One night, during my prayer time, I used some things that I had learned from the word; I decided to talk to God from a different angle. I went to Him and didn't mention anyone else's name. I started with a prayer of repentance, and then I told God the truth about how I felt about ME. I told God the truth about how I felt about my marriage, my husband, my life and everyone else in it, as it relates to ME. I told Him how I'd treated people and how guilty I felt for my actions and decisions. This was the first time that I had heard God so clearly; yes! He told me to… go talk to my husband. I didn't like hearing this; to me, this meant God didn't want to talk to me. I felt God was…rejecting my cry and the pouring out of my heart. What I didn't know was…this was that my prayer had just signed me up for God's class called, "The order of marriage One." God was showing me the order of marriage. God couldn't deal with my pain, at this time, because I was unaware of the order of marriage and had assumed that I only had to talk to God and did not owe my husband any communication of my feelings. Despite my feelings, I obeyed God this time.

I admitted to my husband that I was not sure about the marriage and that I had not wanted it from the beginning. I told him that I had not planned to get married but had grown attached to him. To my surprise, he told me the same. He told me that he felt pressured to marry me. He told me that there was something about me, but he was not in love with me. I also told him that my family had not really approved and he told me that his did not as well. We talked about our first impressions of each other, our faults in the marriage as well as our flaws. I didn't go very deep because I assumed that the "secret things" belonged to God…right? Was I right? Well, if you drive "left," after turning on your "right" turning signal, you could still cause an accident. Sometimes, our well intentions are hidden behind twisted motives, thus God judges the heart…where secret things are hidden. After talking to one another, we decided to talk to God together. We prayed and repented for our deliberate acts of rebellion. We admitted to God that even in our lack of knowledge in some areas, we were still warned before all was destructed. We made a list of everything that we needed from God to change our situation…we needed strength and direction. We told God, in front of each other, that we would do what we had to do to correct this thing. We made a vow to stop fighting the good fight of…fear, as we realized that we had run away from our last home to avoid growing up and facing those who knew we had messed up. Often times, we fight the good fight of "fear," other than fighting the good fight of "faith." As for me and my husband, we asked God, that day for a plan, the power to work that plan, and when/where to implement it. I knew that God had heard me, this time and had forgiven me, but I also knew that I was currently in the midst of the cycle of reaping what I had sown. I didn't expect any answers.

Almost a week later, we decided to go to an evening tent revival. The service was awesome, but I was so dead in spirit, it didn't really matter; I simply felt safe to be in the presence of God's people…I hadn't seen them in such a long time. Near the end of service, a prophet asked my husband to come to the altar and to bring his "wife" with him; I didn't move, initially; I later figured out she was talking to me. She wanted to pray for us. She said that God showed her a vision of us writing down some "requests" and He (God) was going to honor those requests. We went back home feeling rejuvenated and a little encouraged. The problem was, like most people of God when they hear a "word", we went BACK to the same home with the same heart. It wasn't that we didn't believe the word or the prophet; we just believed ourselves to be the masters of sabotaging any good thing that came our way…at least I knew that I did. My memory was my worst enemy at this time and it began to fail me; Oh, I had no trouble remembering things…I just couldn't seem to forget things. I was having trouble forgetting everything and had even started to remember things that had happened to me as a child.

Furthermore, as the prophet had said, a few days later, we did receive some instruction. God told us that he would send money and He would tell us what to do with it. We received the money a couple of days after God spoke to us and He told us to move back to where we had come from. I may have been labeled as a bad decision maker, but at that time, my most precious lesson learned worked in my favor: I had learned how to pray. I learned the lesson of prayer. See, prayer works best when it has a clear stream of honesty to flow from. We pray in amiss when we pray as if God doesn't know the underlying issue. We pray as if God doesn't already know what's going on in our lives. We expect His love to overlook the fact that we are out of order. The blessing and flow may be in Italy, but we expect to reach it in Mississippi. I'm not talking about *Italy* or *Mississippi*…I'm talking about love. We use God's love against Him not knowing that His love doesn't change…His promise just doesn't know where to find you because you're out of place. Another way that we pray in amiss is when we fail to realize that the power in prayer rests in the action taken when we get up from our knees. As for me…I prayed again. I asked God to lead and guide me into the path that He wanted me to go. I confessed to God that I did not know anything about anything, but I did know that I was out if His will. I did some brainstorming and realized where everything had gotten out of order. Somehow, disobedience was the root.

We ended up moving back to Alabama. We didn't know why but we knew there was something about us getting back to our first love…at least we assumed that both of us belonged there. I was satisfied, at this point, that things were going better. Everything wasn't good but…God was speaking to me; this meant a lot to me. This was more priceless to me than silver and gold. I figured, even if God was "fussing" at me, this STILL meant…He was talking to me. In the midst of all of these changes, I could sense a storm in the atmosphere. I knew that I was secretly, still bitter and wondered how anyone could possibly love me, with all that I'd been through. I didn't feel loved or cared for. This was no new feeling for me, but my husband had vowed to love me; he had pledged to take care of me and love me and in my eyes, he had broken that vow. Finally, I had gotten someone to vow and

61

PROMISE to love me, and I…couldn't feel the love. See, I thought if someone vowed, they would…have to love me. The saddest part about the story is, I didn't feel worthy of love. I knew how I felt about me, so I could only but imagine how everyone else loved me.

I feared facing the people who had watched me lose everything that I had, including my sense of direction. I knew that moving back to Alabama would make a statement: I don't make good decisions. Not to mention, I had burned some bridges and had a tendency to write diatribes to those who had hurt me from time to time, which frustrated some so much, they wouldn't even respond. On top of that, I had reached out to people and had poured my heart out to people who did not quite understand who I was…at least that's what I assumed. Maybe they knew…exactly who I was but didn't know that…I had no idea who I was. Sometimes, people expect us to be who they know us to be; when we turn out to be something different from what they thought, they tend to pull back to wait for the rest of us to show up, but can you blame them? How would you have loved me? On the other hand, we label people wrongfully at times. If a person chases us for attention, we assume that they are needy or weird. We fail to realize at times, that wisdom is attractive and a lot of times, they are chasing the anointing that we have. Furthermore, the chaser is well aware of the fact that whatever it is that you have, they do not have and perhaps…they need it.

I knew that I needed help because I knew that my thoughts and understanding were both fuzzy but clear enough for me to "make out" some parts of them; I saw what I wanted to see. Speaking of seeing, I didn't want to see anyone from my past because I felt my reputation had been issued out before the picture developed properly. The way I saw it was, if a person already doesn't understand, fully, who you are, hearing something negative about you paints a clear picture; it doesn't matter if it's true or not…it's just clear. I had heard rumors that I had met this "guy" on the web and ran off to marry him. I make no attacks on web romance, but that story was just not true for me. Sometimes, we are…so glad to be able to say that somebody did us wrong. We want a hater; this makes us feel justified in our actions. I had heard the jokes about me being desperate and needy; this was true, but I needed…Jesus. My whole life, my silence had been translated to weakness and guilt. We all get silent, at times, when we don't know what to say or how to say it. The ridicule though, reminded me of something...something from my past. It reminded me of rejection. I…tucked those feelings away, in my heart, but I didn't put a label on them; somehow, someway…they all got…mixed together in my heart with all of the other pain…or mistakes…or guilt….or, well, at this point, it all looked the same. I had planned to tuck those feelings away, just for a little while and decide, later, if I wanted to forgive them. I never got around to doing that. At this point in my life, my rejection had reached its peak; I was officially living life as if my name was "Rejection." I didn't know where the root of this pain was but I thought of my earthly father often.

My father was a quiet man; if anyone disagrees, it's because I didn't know him as well as you did. I didn't know much about my father, other than the fact that he loved me; I made this assumption based off of the fact that when he did come around, I could feel it. I felt his genuine appreciation for who I was: the person he created. I craved his attention and demanded all of it when he came to visit. I heard things about him but none of those things mattered to me when I was in his presence. I loved my father and often day dreamed about how my life would have been, had he been a part of it. I wasn't sure about "his type" of love, but I wanted it. I felt that he loved me, but I had no proof. I knew that he never meant to hurt me, but I had scars to show me differently. I was raised around my father's family but that didn't take the place of him. It only made me day dream that he was there, if I was around them. Even when he showed up, I wanted him to stay. His family tried to stand in the gap for him, but that only made them…a target for me to display my anger towards him. If I felt rejected by him, I accused them of doing the same; I never said this to them though…I just acted it out.

When I left Alabama, I vowed not to ever come back, but, I didn't know anything about vows though. I was prepared to deal with some people; however, the only person left to deal with was *me*. I didn't quite know all of who I was at this point, but I was right in the midst of doing the *process of elimination*. Sometimes, it takes certain situations to teach you who you are not before you ever come into who you are. I started to see a major commitment problem on my part. I can't tell you anyone's motive; I can only tell you about me…and we're still talking about love.

I noticed how unfaithful and shaky I was and how I couldn't stick to any one task for a long time. I attempted to become active in a ministry and I noticed that I was not dependable. I also noticed

63

how bitter I was; if I even heard the voice of someone who once offended me, my heart would ache, literally. I felt a lot of things, but I never said a word. I went on this way for at least a couple of months. Hiding depression, a failed marriage, bitterness, un-forgiveness and the spirit of fear had become too much for me to bear. I tried my best, though. I couldn't hide behind my smile anymore, because I didn't smile...anymore. Instead, I hid behind valid offense. Valid offense is when you have proof that someone hurt you but you refuse to forgive and you feel justified in holding on. No matter how we "pretty" it up, offense itself is still ugly.

A friend had heard that I was back in town and had offered me a job in my field of study: social work. I took this job, knowing that God had opened this door for me. I knew this, because before, every door had been shut in my face. Things were coming together, but I still felt broken. My rejection and abandonment issues had now been dipped into a sea of bitterness and I couldn't swim. I didn't feel any love for myself anymore and I understood why some others didn't like me as well. How do you love a person like *me*? There I was: hardworking but resentful, thankful but a complainer, loving but unwilling to get close to anyone, favored, yet....rejected by many. How do you love a person like that?

My sense of fashion hadn't always been the norm, but I had my own style. During this time, I dressed as if I didn't care about myself...I didn't care. My bitterness had become verbal; I would go off on people from time to time. Not that they were innocent, but I waited so long from the time they actually did offend me, until it appeared to come out randomly. I tried to restore some relationships, that counted, but the bitter bug would bite me, sometimes in mid-sentence. I couldn't see past what I felt the "world" had don't to me. My relationship with my husband became non-existent because he could no longer reach me. I was working and supporting the family so... I WAS the *man*...boy was I wrong...no pun intended. I wrapped myself into my work and made it my great escape. I flourished on my job because I loved the work that I did...it was also my great escape. My job was the only place where I felt some sense of control. I trusted myself on my job because the work came natural for me; healing someone broken was a pleasure for me. I loved to see SOMEBODY get free; even if I had to "write my book" behind the bars of my own life, I wanted to see people free. I knew that I was trapped within myself and I did not know how to get out.

July 2009, I received some bad news; my father had passed. I didn't know how to feel, at first, because I felt that our relationship had never reached its peak. I felt that things were incomplete between us. We had never made a bond...I mean...let me just be real: I didn't get to tell him how I felt about him not being there. The last time I had seen him was at my college graduation. He had started to reach out to me, a little, when I was in college and I was fearful of his consistency, so I wouldn't allow him to get too close to me. He did try to fix the hole that he knew I had in my heart; what he didn't know was, that hole had become a web. My mother joked about how I could "make" my father move quicker than my other siblings could. I knew that this was because my father knew a secret...he knew that I had his ways...in more ways than one. He knew that I had a hole in my heart. People say, "It takes a man to teach a boy to be a man," but, what does the daughter gain from her father? What does it "take a man" to show his daughter how to be a "what?" A father provides something for his daughter as well and if the father is not there, "she" will also suffer lack in some area. Whatever it "takes a man to teach a women how to be a whatever," she would go lacking in that area. I believe a father provides security and assurance for his daughter; unfortunately, I wasn't very...sure about that. Let's get back to the funeral though.

When I heard of his death, I felt that there were still so many doors left opened and questions unanswered; I was so selfish, his death made me think of all of the things he'd left me to decipher about me. As I sat on the second row at his funeral, I only became more-bitter. After years of yearning for my dad's full attention, I was now sitting on the second row at his funeral...demanding his full attention. I pouted and became angry that he was gone. My two brothers and I all drove our own vehicles to and from the funeral...There was no room in the "family" vehicle. I loved my dad dearly, not to mention I did see him when I looked in the mirror; furthermore, I...didn't know how I felt about my mirror yet. I prayed for God's mercy on my father's soul when he passed and felt a peace that he was in a better place. I began to seek God about my father; God was my only hope in understanding things now. I wanted to know who my father was, what qualities we shared and how he loved me. Don't get me wrong; I knew of my father because my mother made sure that I did. Though I loved him with all of my heart, I never opened up my heart to him...there is a difference. Not to mention, I had a lot of things in my heart, other than love...I loved him with all of "it." When someone says, "I love you with all of my heart," make sure that heart, they are loving you with, is pure or you'll get "loved" with…ALL of their heart. I never told him that I was confused and I never asked for an explanation. I never told him that I craved his attention and I never told him that because of him, I secretly doubted any man's consistency and always trusted a man to…not stand behind his word. I never told my father that I knew he loved me but I didn't know how he loved me. I did tell my father that I loved him every chance I got because a part of me thought that he wondered the same thing about me. I thought of my father often and no foul word(s) spoken against him could ever make me hate him, but I did see him when I looked in the mirror. It was easier to hate the mirror.

My father and I had so many similarities that people noticed: I shake my legs when I'm sleepy and he did the same. He had a monstrous laugh that caught the attention of those around him and I had the same laugh and smile. Lastly, I looked just like him; from the bubbly smile to the mysterious sparkle in my eyes, my father was my mirror. I learned the most about my father after his death…I learned about *me* .In his passing, I learned everything that he had passed on to me. My father was a *quiet* man of many *words*. We may have not been raised in the same home, but the generational traits had made their way to both of our addresses…with no return slip enclosed; I didn't know what to do with the package that had been delivered to me. The thing about generational curses is that they fall upon us all but they land wherever they can find the most room; I left them a front row seat. For example, adultery may run in your family but that doesn't mean that you are bound to be an adulterer; however, if you leave room for adultery in your decision making, you could, more than likely, struggle with adultery. My father had struggled with rejection; I'm not so sure if his voids were ever filled. I knew that my father loved me dearly. He called me "Boot" and I loved it. I never knew why he had given me this name but it made me melt. The older I got, my father kissed my cheek often, when we saw each other. His kiss felt like "guilt" though. I wanted my father to know that I loved him and I'm not sure if he ever really knew. I often wondered why he treated me like his baby girl and why he had such a soft spot for me. I wasn't sure about how he loved me, but I knew he did. I wonder if my father knew that I was in trouble. What if he knew that I was most like him? I knew there were some parts of me that only showed up at "night" but I wasn't sure of what they were because I couldn't name them; it's hard to see clearly when it's dark. By day-light, I didn't want to think about what I had experienced the night before. This sounds like a confession but…we're still talking about love.

My father's passing and my marriage both taught me the nature of a *man*. I had never really understood men before; I just knew that they could and would leave anytime things became uncomfortable for them…that was my understanding. I connected "men" to "rejection." This made any man a …reject before they ever promised to stay. This was unfair to my husband, my brothers, my pastor and any other man in my life. My marriage taught me a lot because my husband had qualities like my father. My father often kissed my cheek when he saw me and my husband did the same. The one thing that scared me was the fact that they both loved me dearly but I couldn't prove it. If someone asked me how I knew, I wouldn't know how to respond; I would say something like, "I can just feel it." They looked at me the same way, though I didn't know how they loved me. I couldn't see past what they both had done to me. I couldn't understand how a person could love someone and not care for them the way they were supposed to. My father never covered me and made me secure; I felt my husband had done the same. The kiss on the cheek made me uncomfortable, at times, because I wanted to get lost in it, but I couldn't find the comfort that I wanted in it. Within my marriage, I learned that I had built a web; I connected everything that happened to me, to my father and my feelings of rejection. I went back to my past, from my childhood all the way to my age at that time. I discovered that I didn't process anything but had grouped everything together. If I was rejected by men, they were "just like my father". If I felt rejected by my family, they were "my father's type". If I was hurt by anyone at any time, I would say, "It doesn't matter because I've seen worst…my own father rejected me". No one could hurt me *better* than my father had already hurt me. These were my thoughts and I rehearsed them every time I had a door shut in my face. The word of God says in Psalms 1, that if a man meditates on God's word day and night, that man will be as a tree planted by the rivers of water. What happens if a man meditates on the pain he/she rehearses, day and night? What type of tree is that man planting? I don't know, but the fruits of my labor, looked like they stemmed from bitter roots. I found myself lost in my own web of rejection. Though my marriage was failing, I was learning so much about who I was not. I was no expert on love…I didn't know how to love or be loved. I didn't know how to love me, which made it impossible to love others the right way.

My marriage taught me some good things; I learned that love covered a multitude of faults. It doesn't matter whose fault it is, when it comes to love. No matter how much I thought about my husband's inconsistency with covering me, I knew that I was no expert in loving him or covering his heart. He had his own flaws and so did I; his were more visible for the world to see. This made him appear to be the only aggressor, to the outside world. His issues were externally exposed and mine were internally decomposed; I was rotting by the day. Even if my flaws were exposed, not every person could label them correctly because my expression was far from the issue. If I snapped, I would appear to be angry; truth was that I allowed things to build up. If I snapped at you, it was because I had allowed you to disrespect me to the point of no return and today was *the day;* also, I was angry. I'm not justifying; this is the truth.

After my father's death, I began to show signs of deep depression and no one could reach me; my illness told me that no one was really trying to and that was partially true. No one wants to be around a negative person and I was not exactly the idea "plus sign". I could day dream for hours, cry for days, and turn my phone off for weeks. I tried going back to work but my memory started to fail me from time to time. I was bitter and felt that every man in my life had treated me like a reject and, of course, my husband was the closet man to me at that time. Losing my father made me more… angry with my father. I felt I never had a chance to express myself to him, get closure, say good-bye or say "hello," for that matter. My husband would pray for me and tell me what God had said; this didn't help because his words didn't carry much weight…my husband's words, I mean…I think…or was that God's word? I would never admit that, if it was. I had grown cold towards my husband; not to mention, he had demonstrated some of his stress to me. "Not providing" was in my web of hurt and he was somehow, caught in the mix. One thing about rejection is, it will keep a person from seeing the whole picture, but it manages to magnify what they think they see. The instability within our marriage had led to our separation. My weight gain, no pun intended, had become another issue and my husband seemed distant. He had started to turn to other means of comfort and I, in return, continued to drown in my sea of rejection. I never blamed him, solely, for the failure of our marriage…I just knew that his issues clashed with mine. We were separated, in spirit, long before our legal separation. From the first day we'd met, we had blamed each other and were turned off. His first impression of me was not good because I had dressed "to impress" and he had so many *red flags* hanging over his head, that I couldn't see who he really was. Driving to see him, when we dated, was an adventure for me and a place to hide because my support system didn't seem so sturdy. My husband and I both escaped in each other, but one couldn't find the other. By this time, my husband had moved back to his hometown and I chose to stay in Alabama. I was left to deal with that person in the mirror: *me.* The pain of the separation forced me to shift my focus; for once in my life, I wanted to have a talk with the person in my mirror. I had learned to talk to God, my husband, even a few other people…but I had never talked to…me. I started to look at how I felt about myself. I wanted to know what "Jewel" felt. Nobody had ever asked how…Jewel feels. Initially, it felt good to hear somebody say, "Jewel, how do YOU feel about things?" I had never asked *Jewel* how she felt or what she wanted. I assumed she just wanted to "not be rejected." At this point, nobody was around to blame, nobody was there to lend me a shoulder to cry on and nobody was bothering me; I felt my world was shattered and I wanted to collect *Jewel.* I wanted to know how *Jewel* loved me…at times, I felt as if she didn't love me. I realized quickly that…we didn't know each other. I didn't know who I was. I began to search the word, to see what God had said about me. I wanted to find out who I was to God, my purpose and how I'd gotten to this *point* in my life. See, it's impossible to know who you are if you don't know the person who created you to be you. A lot of times, when we come through traumatizing situations in our lives, we fail to realize that we may have lost parts of who we are. Some loss is good but some is not. It's always beneficial to evaluate where you are in the process so that you can decide if you need to be *emptied out, mixed or refilled.* It's never wise to throw away every part of you just because something is not working properly. Sometimes, our hearts get overwhelmed and need to be emptied out completely, so that God can fill the heart again. Other times, some things have lost "flavor" and simply need to be mixed together after God adds salt or pepper. We don't always know how to measure but God does. Furthermore, there are times when we are depleted and God needs to refill us again; we have allowed too many things/people/places to cloud our hearts, and God has to empty us completely out, just to be able to see that we still have a heart. Only God can create a clean heart within us; we can't do this ourselves because we may take away, empty or delete something that needs to be "fixed" and placed in the proper place. As for me at this particular time in my life, I had so many twisted views of who I was, what I had done and how God felt about me, I needed to be completely emptied out, mixed and refilled…all at the same time, before any new knowledge could even stick. I needed a clean heart AND a renewed mind. At the age of 28, I wanted to know what I was and what made God refuse to let go of me. I assumed that He was holding on to me because I was still standing, with no power of my own. I wanted to know why God refused to let me die. I was tired of feeling like a failure and I was tired of allowing people to define who I was…even if the loudest person of influence was me. There's nothing wrong with being labeled by those who care; however, the only catch is, those same people can strip you of the title that they've placed on you, as soon as you show them a different side of you…IF, what they call you is your "only name." I decided, at this time in my life, to disown and disconnect from everything that I had thought about myself, everything that I'd ever been told and I began to search myself. I even explored the smallest details about me; I wanted to know why I hated for people to leave my home or any place without saying good-bye. I knew that I had always hated that, but had never explored how it made me feel or why I felt that way. I asked myself to tell me how this made me feel. My mirror answered: "When someone leaves your home without telling you that they're gone, it makes you feel like they either discovered something more important than saying good bye, or they didn't think enough of your presence to dismiss themselves properly." This came from my interpretation of how my father had left…years ago. The next question was: "What are YOU thinking when YOU leave someone without saying good-bye?" WAIT A MINUTE!! I DIDN'T ASK THAT QUESTION!! The voice of God had invaded my thoughts! Finally, I had heard Him as clear as day! God crossed examined all of my questions with His own questions. I answered: "Well, I don't leave people's homes without saying good bye...well, maybe a few times. I wasn't thinking about how it would make them feel; I felt I had spent time with them and I knew that I would see them again. Sometimes, the person would be doing something that I felt was important and I didn't want to disturb them from that "thing" by saying good-bye." God asked, "Why do you always conclude the worst?" I answered, "I don't know…I'm used to it though." I began to read about God to see why he chastened me so much. When He did speak, it felt like a rebuke; I wanted Him to love me a different way. I read in His word that He chastened those that He loved; the word compared this to a "father to son" relationship. "God, are you saying, you ARE my Father?" I began to feel the love of *God, the Father.* This is when I learned that God loved me so much that, He ran the risk of having me "accuse" Him of rejecting me, just so He could *Father* me. Was it true that God loved me so much that He was not intimidated by my faults or flaws? He continued to *Father* me, even when He knew I'd label Him as "The One who rejects me?" I continued to collect Jewel's but this one was most dear to me. I was not fatherless; God was my Father.

One thing that stood out to me was my prayer life. I realized that prayer had always been a part of my life; even when I didn't know how to pray, I had prayed for God to teach me. Poetry and writing were also my passions, though I hadn't fully embraced either. I studied my writing style and noticed how free I felt when I had a chance to release my thoughts and feelings in rhyme. I allowed myself to flow freely in those three things just to see how far I would go: I prayed without ceasing, I wrote whatever came to mind, and I wrote at least two poems a day for a couple of months. I even used my past mistakes to help me understand "me;" I went back to look at my "diatribes" that I had written to people that I felt had hurt me…I turned them all into poems. I found that this too was misplaced passion. The diatribes were not of God; the unction to write was. It still hurt me to know that…I'd hurt other people with my writing. My gift had not made room for me, so I sat on top of other people. I didn't know before but I could see clearly now: I had a skill for writing that the enemy had used against me. God showed me how everybody had "things" to deal with and we all could find healthy ways to release hurt and pain. I was not proud of my diatribes, but the pain that promoted those scrolls was real. I healed through my writing. A harsh truth is, sometimes in life we have to face the fact that we just might be as hard to love as we think we are. It's hard to love a person who works hard to convince you that they are… unlovable. Learning to love yourself is a process if you've never loved yourself before. Each exploratory measure taken to get to know you better is worth the time. I was interested in *Jewel,* who she was, and fascinated day by day as more of "me" came out. I was finally…collecting Jewel. I was now convinced that any person, who felt they didn't like their self, had never met their true self before and only hated the character(s) that they were portraying to be.

Another thing that I tried to do, during my separation, was change my appearance. I wanted something new and different; I felt a need to find "my look". It wasn't quite time for that though because I started wearing long weaves and artificial ponytails. Everyone was wearing those, at that time, and I felt a need to prove that I could do it too. That look didn't last long because the pony tails broke my hair off and the weaves looked good to everyone else, but not to me…I wasn't satisfied with that look. I looked "the part" but it didn't make me happy. I didn't want to develop more issues with trying to fit the mold. Beauty shines from the inside out. I never fully understood that saying, although I'd heard something similar before; I was learning that the more I learned about who I was on the inside, the more I desired to reward my outside by fixing "her" up. I desired to lose weight and shop for clothes that fit my body well. The more God revealed to me about who I was, the more I desired to look better. I stopped rehearsing my past; I made a conscious decision to "stop telling my story." A lot of people get confused with the scripture in the bible that compels us to share our testimony in order to free others. If there is still pain and confusion attached to the story, it has not yet developed into a testimony…it's only a test and nobody is to talk in the middle of a test; the "teacher" will accuse you of cheating and you may even get a zero or have points deducted…right? During the storm, we are instructed to be still and know (Psalm 46: 10) and after the storm, we are to testify about how we made it out so others will be made strong by our testimonies.

I began to fall for myself; I didn't just…fall; I fell in love. I didn't quite trust my "consistency" but I was secretly falling for the person in my mirror. The first thing I became attracted to was my name; I studied *Jewel*. I realized that God had named me Jewel long before I had ever made my first mistake or before I made my first "on purpose." Every failure is not a mistake; some things we do (have done) on purpose. None the less, God called me "Jewel"; not only was I precious to Him, but He called me Jewel before I was shaped or molded to fit any form; He had chosen me and had named me what He wanted me to be called: I was *Jewel* on purpose. God had not made a mistake in naming me. He had never called me *out of my name.* Even when I changed my name, He had still called me *Jewel.* I would love to tell you that I stopped thinking of my past, but that wouldn't be true. The truth is, it was a process, but I had started to change my thinking. I could think about something else other than my flaws. I constantly had flashbacks of my past. I tried praying the thoughts away, but my memory had always proven to be one of my strengths and I had learned enough about prayer to know that prayer didn't work that way. When it comes to our past, prayer will, at times, stand behind you to make you strong enough to deal with or handle your past…not take it away. I had finally figured out that I was not expected to forget my past or who I once was. I started challenging myself to reduce the pain attached to my past so that the very life of the situation would starve to death. I created a plan of action: I decide that every time I had a thought or flashback of my past, I would talk to "it". I started telling my spirit that I took full responsibility for who I once was, but I was not what I'd done nor was I what I had been through…I told my past that my name was *Jewel* and that's the name that I would answer to. I reminded myself of who I was not and a little of who I was. I knew a little about who I was, but I knew more about who I was not. I was not a failure and I was not rejected by God; I was not ugly and I was not a screw up. I told myself that I was a writer, an intercessor and a child of God…these were the only sure things that I knew so far. If my memory bank "wrote out a check in my old name", I still signed the back of the check with my new name: *Jewel*. At times, I could convince myself without struggle, while on other days my past used my own tactics against me. My past would remind me of who I was, what I had done and how unsure I was about things, most of the time. I told my past that I was aware of that but this time, God said it…not me. During my process, I would have flashbacks of scenes in my life; times when I allowed others to use me, knowingly. I was reminded of how much of a pushover I was and how I had allowed myself to be used in my past. Those memories were the hardest to fight off because they made me feel insignificant and often times stirred up feelings of anger. I had rehearsed things before, but at this time in my life, I felt the pain during the rehearsal, but I had the strength to encourage myself. I told myself that I was not the tail though I appeared to be the butt of everyone's joke(s). It's hard to see yourself as the head and not the tail when you always seem to finish last…but who says when it's the "end"? How can you always finish last when the race is not done yet? I stopped focusing on why so many people had walked out and I continued to search for more reason why God chose to stay. I realized that I had been viewing myself as a messed up individual versus an individual who messed up. I became convinced that God must've still seen me as *Jewel* because He had never turned me over to any other name. I admitted to myself, and to God, that I could have been justly labeled as a lot of things just by my curiosity alone, but God had blocked it and I was still "Jewel". He chose to still call me by my name; the least I could do was answer to the call. I began to thank God for my upbringing… struggles and all because they had all made me "Jewel". They say the thing that doesn't kill you will ultimately promote strength and that may be true; however, I would not be "Jewel" if I didn't see it another way. We quote that saying as if the strength is gained in the ability to still remain standing after the striking of the weapon or blow. I believe that the strength is found in the way we process things after and during the battle as well as what we choose to learn from it. I changed my whole way of thinking; I sought out to study my ability to overcome certain situations verses rehearsing the damage that it had done to me. Another deception of rejection is that it causes a person to become focused on all that has (had) happened to them so that they won't realize that they are the over comer. Most things were designed to kill, yet we (over comers) managed to live through them. My mirror started to look a little better. I started to like my mirror; it was a little clearer. I was not my past, but it was a part of who I was. I was not lost, although every puzzle piece was not yet in place. I had not collected all of "Jewel" but I had a visual of who she was meant to be.

The next thing I studied was my heart, because from it flowed the issues of my life; not to mention my bible suggested that God would judge me from this place. Everything that I found in my heart was not good. I found a lot of selfishness there. I learned that one of my pet peeves was being misunderstood. I used to blame others for not understanding me, but I failed to realize that I lacked some communication skills. If you ever want to measure your growth and maturity, see how much you can admit about your faults. I thought about my marriage and other relationships that I had…not being clear was something that I had been accused of several times. I hated this accusation because it made me feel less of who I thought I was…if there was such a thing. Well, before you feel sorry for me, let me admit that during my discovery, I found that I was not always clear and I did not always have the right words to say. I had a gift for writing but that had little to do with my communication skills. I began to practice being clear and honest. I told my boss at work to let me know if any speaking engagements came up because I wanted to be the one to speak. I wasn't very clear with her, no pun intended, about why I wanted to speak, so I don't think that went over too well. My eagerness to speak could have been translated as a threat to take someone else's job. I didn't bother explaining; I knew that the time would come and things would flow smoothly. I began scheduling group meetings with all of my clients weekly so that I could speak to larger groups of people to practice and test my communication skills; I did evaluation forms so that I could get feedback. The feedback was awesome, but I noticed something; I didn't have a problem being clear…I had an honesty problem. My clients became confused when I added "sugar" to things that didn't need "sugar" added. Most of my clients said that they were confused when I was not blunt about a reprimand; it was hard for me to give harsh truths face to face. I took that constructive criticism and taught myself to be honest and tactful at the same time. Honesty has to be practiced, at times, if you've grown accustomed to hiding your true self. I didn't like to lie; I was afraid of the truth…I was afraid that other's wouldn't like me, if I told a harsh truth…I was afraid of being disliked…I was afraid of rejection; this made me more prone to tell the truth in pieces. I began to practice telling the truth, even if nobody wanted to hear it. I practiced at work. Instead of getting my boss to talk to my groups about keeping their rooms clean, I volunteered to do so. I didn't like the fact that I could see several residents rolling their eyes as I spoke to them…but I did like the fact that they…cleaned their rooms and thanked me later for warning them before they lost their place in the program. The "truth" not only sets us free but it also leaves the door open for others to follow in our footsteps. It's selfish to be untruthful; we are untruthful at times because we want to please others…but, it's not about them. We want them to be pleased so we can continue to be "liked." This is selfish.

It's impossible to overcome the spirit of rejection without acknowledging the fact that you may have some qualities about you that make people a little uncomfortable with you. People who love you are uncomfortable when you aren't honest about your faults and you are not approachable for them to help you; rejection causes one to be unclear about his/her feelings and that person will only see what "they" feel. On the other hand, people who don't love you will quickly tell you where to go and remind you that you are wasting their time. See, during my search, some things that I found in my heart did not look like God; I hated those things and I prayed for God to take those things away. Some things, He did take just as soon as I let them go, but other things he didn't take. I asked God to make me bolder because I hated being sensitive. The boldness came, but the sensitivity stayed. From that, I learned that I was not only sensitive to my emotions, but I was also sensitive to the emotions of others, as well as their needs. God needed me to stay this way. I could tell if a person was hurting and no smile could easily fool me. God had made me this way; it was a part of who I was; He needed me to be sensitive to the needs of others. He needed me to be sensitive, but He didn't intend for me to be consumed with sensitivity. God places some things in us, but He never intended for those "things" to dominate us. You may have a giving heart but God did not intend for you to be overtaken by giving. This would cause you to give away things that He didn't permit you to give away. I searched my heart to find out what had perverted His intentions: I found *offense* there. It's so easy to become bound by offense when you don't know who you are. We have all been offended at some point in our lives, but mistaken identity may cause a person to become stuck in a particular place or time. I made a decision not to take things personal unless they were; with that, I made a decision not to be offended…as simple as that. My "new" expression was, "You aint' talkin' to me IF you aint' talkin' to me." This meant that I would not assume that someone meant me harm or was trying to say something to hurt me IF they didn't direct their comments to me. This did away with paranoia; Offense comes with paranoia. When we are offended, we become professional "people readers." Even if a person doesn't say anything to us, we assume that we know what they are thinking. I made a decision to mind my own business and retire my *professional people reading* degree that I'd obtained from the school of hard knocks.

Almost (love) doesn't count

My mirror was starting to take on a different form and I was becoming very attracted to it. Although I thought about my husband often, marriage was still a sensitive area for me. I knew that the marriage wouldn't work because we were not willing to make it work, but I hated divorce as much as I hated broken families. Broken families symbolized *failure* to me. Broken families symbolized...being alone, to me because, I had run everyone else away. I loved my husband and I cared for his well-being, but I knew the marriage was not true from the beginning. My husband symbolized my past and I wanted no more parts of my past. I felt my marriage had caused me to act out of character...whoever I was at that time. I had done some things that I wasn't proud of and I couldn't quite get over myself...or whoever I was at that time. After two separations and much counsel, I decided to go through with the divorce. I also left my husband that year; I'm sure you thought that was a typo, but it was not. I got a divorce that year...and I left my husband also; those are two separate things. Divorce is the legal process; becoming unattached to the pain and situation completely, is a whole different thing. Most people divorce but they don't leave. I did them both. I also divorced my past. I gave God all of me. My husband's flaws had little to do with the divorce, contrary to popular belief. I couldn't deal with the choices I had made, decisions I'd made and the consequences that had followed. I had to deal with the consequences of my decisions and some choices made "themselves". When we choose NOT to deal with our own issues, somehow, someway, they are dealt with...with or without our approval. There is always an "outcome" to any situation, whether we make a decision or not. It's often assumed that divorcees are "advocates" for divorce. I am not. Divorce is an ugly thing and God loves marriage and family. If I were asked to give my take on divorce, I wouldn't speak from that angle because I don't have a "take;" divorce is not an option, even though it has become a common outcome. Divorce is permitted, in some instances, and I wouldn't release myself from a marriage, without those "grounds" to stand on. As for my "take," I would take marriage seriously. I would encourage that individual to learn about marriage before entering into it. Marriage is not the proposal, the wedding day, the cake or the dress...I never had either. Marriage is the coming together of two complete people, with two different lives to build one life together on Godly foundation. The bible talks about adultery being one thing that releases us from marriage; if that's not you OR if you've chosen to continue past the adultery, make it work. If you have had (or if you are well on your way) to a failed marriage, it may benefit you more to process your single life and your past relationships as a whole. Ask yourself some questions. Whether you are divorced, separated, in the process or still believing God to restore the marriage/relationship, use your time to fall in love with God again so that you'll be completely open to his healing, his love, his rebuke and/or His instructions. Crying over what happened, what didn't happen, and/or what should have happened will not help the process. Forget about your "critics" during your time. The toughest critics are those who have never been where you are. Do some self-reflections, your choices and your decisions...your patterns, your tendency to not want to be alone. Sometimes, we just don't like to be alone and we don't want to admit that. Are you content in a quiet house where the only voice you hear is God's? Could you hear God's voice if it was just you and Him? What do you think about when you're alone? What place were you in, in your life when your ex. came into your life? What place was she/he in? Not just a physical place, but what path were you on? Were you in the season of sewing or reaping? Waiting or "already waited?" What did God say about the relationship? Did you ask Him? Did you wait for His response? Was His response confirmed by someone (spiritual) that you trusted at the time? Think on those things. In doing so, you may even fall in love with you and get the revelation that most people don't get when they find themselves in divorce court: **"You don't have a problem being married; you had a problem being SINGLE or you have a problem being married BECAUSE you had a problem being single. Some of the most failed marriages are the result of people who hated being single. Single is not just a "status;" it's a point in the process of marriage. Marriage is for those who have gone through the "process" of being single.** I may not be an expert on marriage, but I can surely tell you about the importance of being single, valuing that time, and keeping yourself. Those are all areas that I've had the most of my struggles in and lessons to learn. I'm not an expert; I'm an over comer with a testimony. We're not talking about *divorce,* though; we're still talking about love. Let's get back to the process.

I evaluated my interactions with others and my judgment of character; at first, I thought that I was not a good judge of character because I often surrounded myself with people who I thought were my world, when in actuality, they were never meant to even be a part of it. What I discovered about me was that I was an awesome judge of character...I just chose to play an "awkward" character of my own: I *played* dumb. I wasn't always blind- sided. When I looked back, I could see that I often knew exactly what "could" happen to me, even if I didn't believe that it could happen to me. I could no longer use the excuse that I was "caught off guard;" I learned that I was still not…very honest, even with what I felt about someone.

I began to reach out to some family members and restore some broken relationships. What I found was that God can restore, but we decide how we deal with the person even after restoration. We also decide if the person who hurt us is worth our time. We can choose to forgive and forget the person or we chose to forgive and forget what the person has done to hurt us. Either way, it's our choice and we're in good standing. We have to allow others to make that choice as well. I learned that people will forgive you but they won't forget the lesson that you taught them. It's easy to accuse someone of doing us wrong when they decide to cut us out of their lives completely after they forgive us; they have the right to choose where to place you once you step…out of the place they initially had you. Example: if a friend loved you so much that they call you "sister," then you hurt them, that friend might forgive you, but you can't get upset if you are moved from being called "sister" to "associate." YOU stepped out of line. They welcomed you back in but your actions moved you to a different place in their lives. As for me, I made a choice, during the big separation, to forgive others, apologize and forget whose fault it was; it didn't matter anymore because love would cover the whole multitude of faults…both mine and theirs. I was willing now, to love them from whatever angle they wanted me to.

I read my bible day and night consistently because God would always meet me there and I needed Him to meet me at least "half way". I began to accept the fact that God did not see me the same way that I'd seen myself for the past years of my life. God taught me to hear His voice. One morning, I was headed to work with little money to last me to the next pay period. God spoke to me and told me not to put any gas in my car. I was already at a half of tank but it would not make it to the next pay period; I didn't know why, but I had planned to use my last to purchase the gas because I knew that I had to be able to get to work for the rest of the week. God told me that He would send someone to give to me what I needed. I had other options, but I chose to trust God. Don't get me wrong, I was always fairly sensitive to God's voice, but it would only take minutes before I doubted that it was even

Him speaking to my spirit, in the past. Once I made it to work, I didn't think much about what God had said because I became busy with work. Near the end of the day, a co-worker came into my office and attempted to hand me money; she told me that God had instructed her to give to me. My pride led me to give it back to her, but she explained to me that my refusal to receive would cause her to become dishonest and disobedient and she would not allow me to make her miss her blessing. God had kept His word, but I learned that day that God was not talking about money when He said someone would "give to me;" my co-worker had given me wisdom. The money was a token but the lesson was the gift. That day, I learned that my tendency to be prideful was not cute and had destroyed a lot of my relationships and cut off a lot of blessings…both for me and others around me. I realized that I had been too prideful in my marriage and had not expressed to my husband or anyone else just how hurt I really was. I knew it was only fair that my husband knew the truth; I knew that he needed to know that although the marriage was not joyful, I had lived most of my life without real joy. I wanted him to know that I had to walk away, but it was not because of him alone. I learned, that day, that pride really did come before destruction. I realized that I had not been as "real" as I had claimed to be. I never admitted my hurt, I never admitted when I was wrong, but instead, I cut people off and distanced myself in the name of "letting them breath" when the truth was…I did not want to face the issue. I even thought about the fact that I had trained my body to swallow tears; I could force myself not to cry if I didn't want to be vulnerable. I felt a release that day; God had used my co-workers mouth to teach me a valuable lesson…not to mention, my gas tank was now on full and so was my pocket book, thanks to her; I felt like I could go a little further now…literally.

I was so excited, I vowed not to ever hurt anyone else again…HOW MANIPULATIVE! Sometimes, we say things to justify our actions and that's all a part of the spirit of rejection. Saying such things make us feel better and justified but beneath the surface, they are lies and we know who the father of lies is. The enemy leads us to make promises instead of decrees; there is a difference. Decrees are those things we declare, announce or speak; when we decree, we are speaking a thing, and heaven backs us up. Promises are different; they have more to do with our own ability and might; they cannot be trusted. We feel no one has a right to doubt us when we promise. If we make a promise to someone, we secretly dare them to doubt us and that's deception. In my case, the truth was, I didn't want to be hurt by hurting someone again and I didn't want to be vulnerable. Both of those things are a part of life. It would have benefited me more to tell God my fears and allow Him to show me how to deal with adversity, instead of washing them away.

Speaking of washing, everyone has that one thing that relaxes them from a long day or prepares them for a long day ahead: mine was bathing. I loved to take baths. Bath time was my think time. I took baths both morning and night. I loved to sit in water with bubbles and simply think. One morning, I woke up and was feeling really down. I knew that I had decisions to make and I didn't trust me to make those decisions alone. I had been spending time with God, getting to know myself and had learned just how messed up I really was; at the same time, God was healing me. This particular morning, I got in the tub and began to weep, hysterically. God spoke to me, while I was in the tub, and told me to wash my "hands". I started washing my hands vigorously. I didn't understand what He was saying to me, but I did it. I felt a little "loony" because I had never heard of anyone who washed their hands, as if they were about to eat, while in the bathtub. God then spoke to me and said, "Don't assume that your "hands" are clean just because you used them to wash the rest of your body." I wasn't clear about what God was saying to me, but it felt like a rebuke. I searched the word to find out what this meant. In the bible, Matthew 24, I found that washing ones hands symbolized "innocence". We assume, at times, that just because God is on our side, cleansing us and making us a new creature, it means that we are totally innocent in the situation. This is not so. God's forgiveness, and perhaps the forgiveness of others, makes us "not guilty" and no one has the right to hold anything over our heads; however, that does not change facts. The facts may prove that you are guilty; with God, we don't carry the weight of that guilt...He carries for us. If we are not careful though, we will walk around like God saved us because we did NO wrong. If we are not careful, we will mistake the grace over our heads, for a "queen's crown." The facts may also carry consequences and that's not punishment. Just because you are "not guilty" that doesn't mean you "did nothing wrong." God's "not guilty," means you may not be innocent, but you are "forgiven," just as if it didn't happen. This still doesn't mean your hands are clean enough to feed your neighbor before washing your hands. As for me, God had saved me but I wasn't innocent. I no longer had blood on my hands, but that didn't mean there was no blood; the salvation meant that the blood was now placed over my head.

Consequences are like side effects to medicine; they are the result of something that went down much easier than it comes back up. It's easy to mess things up and allow pride to lead you into places. Once God delivers you, you might not smell like smoke, but that doesn't change the "fact" that you WERE in the fire. God demonstrated to me, that day, that He was cleaning me up, but I was not justified in my poor decision making. He didn't clean me because I was…better than my husband. He cleansed me because HE was God.

Unconditional Love

Now, I know that this is normally the part of "the book" where I'm supposed to tell you that once I learned who I was, the whole world treated me differently. You may want me to tell you that my husband and I reunited and everything was perfect thereafter. I'm sure you're waiting on the part where I confronted that childhood bully and we became the best of friends. You want me to tell you that my family and I get along perfectly now and we have reunions once a month. I know that I would love to tell you that I finally figured out why my father left my mother alone with the responsibility of raising me and my siblings; it would also be my pleasure to tell you that I understand why I sat on the second row at my dad's funeral. If I could tell you those things, it would, perhaps, make it…easier for you to "love me." It would be a perfect ending…but this is not a story, nor is it the end. I don't know where my childhood bully is and I don't think about her. I can tell you that the spirit of rejection is an ongoing temptation for me but it's no longer a struggle. I can tell you that I am…a child of God. In case you just missed that, this is my happy ending. See, the root of my bitterness was rejection. I "found the Father." I finally believed that God, not only loves me but He chose me to be a vessel for him. See, God's "I love you" is not a general statement. When God says, "I love you," He's saying, "I love what I created!" When God says I love you, "He's saying it WITH the knowledge of who you are…good and bad. We can hide things from those around us and assume they love us because of what they…don't know. I don't know how you would love me if I…walked you through every phase of my childhood and marriage. I left some things unspoken because…we're talking about *love*. If you knew some things I've gone through, you would feel sorry for me by now and, we're not talking about feeling sorry…we're talking about love. When God says, "I love you," He's saying: "I love MY (shy, short, chubby, dark, smiley, moody, curious, funny, mean at times, rude at times, untrusting at times, untrustworthy at times, struggling at times, not as smart as she looks, beautiful but doesn't know it at times, loving, caring, fragile, sensitive, friendly, overly-talkative at times, quiet at times, unsure, uneasy) *Jewel!*" God's "I love you" goes far beyond what I want Him to think of me. I learned why God loved me; in all these things, I am still a conqueror because God loves me. He named me *Jewel* before my life gave me any other name. GOD HAD NAMED ME! This made me happy. I started to have a desire to be just who He said I was. The more I learned about me, the more I became humble that God had made it a little easier for me than most…or did He?? I say this because people search a lifetime trying to figure out who God wants them to be…but, my name said it all. God made me *Jewel* and that's who He wanted me to be. I stopped looking for answers and questions. We create questions when we demand answers for things that were simply created to just…be. Some questions will be answered along the way, while in route to destiny and others may never be answered. I became content with what I knew and I demanded my mind and soul to love the person in the mirror. She was not her faults, she was not her father and she was not pain…she was always *Jewel*. God said so.

After I learned to love myself, I had assumed that I was the only person in love with *me* but the more I loved myself, the more I started to…love others and open myself up to be loved. With "self-hate" out of the way, I was able to see clearly, the love from others. I met a friend who helped me to deal with some tough times; my choices had left me with some consequences and I was now constantly having anxiety attacks that made me feel as if I was suffocating…at least twice a day. I accepted the "attacks" and had assumed that I would just have to learn to live with them. The way I saw it was, I had lived with the spirit of rejection for over 27 years; my thinking would not change overnight. We can be healed and forgiven within a matter of seconds, but it takes a lifetime of commitment to redirect our thought process. I became so focused on the word of God, that I literally scared the…panic attacks away. I made a decree that I would read the word every time I felt a panic attack coming on; I did just that and those attacks slowly but surely, went away.

I'm not ashamed of my past and will talk about it openly. I may be judged harshly by thousands but the other 30 who are delivered by MY word of testimony mean so much more to me. There is always a lesson in any storm for us because we can't learn for other people; even if you were hurt or done wrong, the lesson is still meant for you. Sometimes, our feelings can be deceiving. I want to share something God taught me throughout my battle with rejection and abandonment issues. During the healing process, God taught me to identify HIS voice in my thought process. He told me to use, what I now call the process of "truth or dare". This is where you question yourself. Questioning yourself is much different from "second guessing yourself". Question your thoughts. My questions went something like this: My mind would make a suggestion: "The whole world is crashing down on me!" My question: "Is that possible…physically or mentally?" If the whole world crashed down on me, physically or mentally, I would be dead; I am not God and I cannot carry the weight of the world on my shoulders. I then realized that if God didn't say it, it had to be a lie...and the devil is the father of lies, so it was easy to identify the father of that *baby*. If your thoughts are not "true," dare yourself to meditate on them. Truth or dare?

I challenge you, today, to listen to yourself and question your thoughts, even when your "mind" says, "I can't do this", whatever "this" is, you know that God didn't say that because He can't lie and the Word of God, already says that you could do ALL things through Him. Don't you dare believe the lies that the enemy plants in your mind; however, keep in mind that he can ONLY plant those things...it is up to you to water those plants, feed those plants or let them die. It's not as bad as you "think" and if it feels that way, you may need to redirect your thoughts.

When I evaluated my thought process, I found...a lot of voices in my mind, but none of them sounded like God. Sometimes, they sounded like "me" and other times, they sounded like someone who had hurt me in my past. Learning to redirect your thoughts helps you to learn to hear God clearly even in a crowded room. Our mind can be the most crowded place, at times. The mind is where we harbor and rehearse things we've heard in the past, concerning who we are or what others think of us. We don't have to guess how God feels about us or how he loves us; He's already declared His love for us. One thing really amazed me: I used to have the most "conversations" with my thoughts while sitting in church service. I had assumed that God chose to speak to me in service because it was the best time that He could reach me...not through the preacher, but through my own thoughts. My mind would say some "real" stuff to me, during church service, but the thoughts distracted me from the message being preached and from enjoying service. One day (while I was NOT in church), God spoke to me and said; "Why would I talk to you DURING the church service? If I did talk to you during church service, what would be the purpose of you going to hear the word if you already have the answer inside of your "mind?" I said, "..but God, what my mind was saying was true!" God reminded me of HIS encounter with the enemy when He was tempted and the devil said true things to Him at the wrong time (See Mathew 4). For years, I had gotten my most "revelations" of MY life IN church and was blown away to find that God was not the one speaking to me...a little scary, huh? Maybe the enemy doesn't speak to you in church but whenever he speaks to your thoughts, you can now identify Him by this one true fact: God CANNOT lie...the devil CAN'T stop lying. Even if the devil tells you something true, watch for the spirit of confusion; the enemy's truths leave us confused and hopeless. God's rebuke even brings comfort; God chastens those that He loves. God won't chastise you without loving you all at the same time.

I denounced every "accessory" that came with the suit of oppression. Our issues come with a *survival* kit; I call them survival kits because they are the things that come with our issues, in order for the issue to stay alive. Sometimes, the accessories in the survival kit, are harder to shake than the actual issue. A person might get delivered from lying but may be left with a manipulative nature. In order to be a good liar, no pun intended, a person has to be able to manipulate others; the spirit of lying might leave, after deliverance, but the person may now have to check their motives when trying to persuade others to make sure they are not operating under manipulation. Depression also comes with a *survival kit:* anxiety, promiscuity, doubt, stubbornness and selfishness...to name a few. In order to be depressed, you have to learn to make everything about you; this is where selfishness is bred. Selfishness can go undetected or unnoticed because even those who reach out to people who are depressed, want to know what is going on with YOU, who hurt YOU, how do YOU feel and how can they help YOU? After we are healed from depression, we now have to challenge ourselves to think about someone other than *self.*

In God, I found my meaning and I could make sense of life. I learned how to love wholeheartedly in the most challenging places to love. I accepted the fact that I was not a mistake and neither were the things that I'd seen. From my failed marriage to the city that I lived in, God had allowed it all. Yes...we are still talking about Love.

My best friend brought me to her family and they called me *family.* They never knew that she was ministering to me and was showing me how to love and be loved. I admired her family. Nobody ever asked me who I was, where I came from, or what "my story" was. They welcome me into the family and overwhelmed me with love. Even if they asked for my story, nobody asked me. Every so often, I would have these times where I would try to pull away; my past would remind me that people could walk out on you whenever they chose to, so it would not be good to become attached. God would use my friend to remind me that they chose to love me. I called them my God family because God had given them to me. They made me…appreciate my blood family. My family was different from theirs but I loved my blood family more than ever now. I didn't want them to be like my blood family and I didn't want my blood family to be like them…the difference was good. I began to love and appreciate the fact that God had chosen me to be a "Moore." I was not placed in my family by accident or incident; God had done this thing on purpose. I began to thank God for my mother, all she'd taught me, the struggles we'd seen (they made us stronger) and my two brothers. I was grateful for my God-family; I was thankful for my blood family. God knew what He was doing when He gave them both to me. It's always important to remember that God does nothing out of "boredom;" we do this at times. When God placed you in your family, He did so because you all need something from one another. That "thing" that you're missing may be because your brother or sister is the only one who can give that "thing" to you. Everything God does is for the sake of building the kingdom of God. Your sister is not just someone that looks like you, talks like you and loves you unconditionally; your sister may also be your "God-given" prophet: "And He gave some apostles; and some prophets, and some evangelists; and some pastors and teachers, for the perfecting of the saints, for the work of ministry, for the edifying of the body of Christ." Ephesians 4:11-12. Your mother is not just the person who birthed you; she could also be your personal, God-given evangelist. This is one reason the bible encourages us to know them that labor amongst us; if we knew the purpose of those in our families, we would not throw them away so easily. I value my family. Maybe you're saying, "Well, my family is not close and I've never met my mother." I understand and this may be true for you. Allow me to encourage you to scan your circle. Who has God placed in your life to be a voice for Him? Somebody has reached out to you, somebody has told you about the Lord and somebody is praying for you. If you can't identify who God has given you, start by identifying who…God is. Let's collect some more Jewel's.

As for me, I started to look better on the outside too; I found a love for natural hair and I stopped relaxing my hair; it was my look. I make no attacks on the relaxing system but, this natural thing is for me. I know what you're thinking; what does hair have to do with love? Maybe nothing! I LOVE hair and hair creations. Okay…now, we are talking about love. There was something about seeing "me," in my natural state that led me to appreciate God more for the little things. My natural hair was more beautiful than any other artificial piece of hair that I'd ever worn on my head. When I combed my hair, I thanked God for the ability to grow hair. When I had a bad hair day, I thanked God that I had "hair" on my head. I learned to thank God for everything that He'd naturally given me. Even for the people in my life, I thanked God for them. The more I trusted God, the more I trusted His people. I realized that I was not just an "o.k." person but I was as beautiful as God had made a woman to be. When God said, "I will create a help meet suitable for HIM," God was talking about "me." I was fearfully and wonderfully made. I was built to "help meet" the needs of God first, and my husband (at a set time). I wasn't missing any parts because He had already covered my imperfections and He was not taken by surprise by my life's happenings. Sometimes, we react in fear as if God is having to "come up with some ideas" for our lives, on the spot. God is not shocked about the fact that you were laid off from your job; He already wrote out a plan. It's up to you to seek Him and work the plan. God's word tells us that God knows the beginning from the end (Isaiah 46:10). We don't always know the beginning and we can't know the end; all we know is what God has said and what we see; for all else, we walk by faith. While you are walking, what does all of this mean for our love walk? All of who we are and all that we have experienced shapes the way we view love and the way we love. Why is love so important? Love is that "thing" that God has commanded us to do; on the contrary, love is that "thing" that we don't do freely. We give love and take it away, as if we have the option to NOT love. To understand and learn to love again, we must first define love: Love is a "command" not a "demand." God commands us to love, not to demand it. When we demand love, we assume that someone else owes it to us. When we understand that love is made, created and given by God, we will understand that we receive it freely, we give it whole-heartedly and we deserve it. GOD is love. Now, that's not just a *phrase.* Love is not your fluffy feelings, however, some feeling is needed in order to keep love alive. Remember, a few verses up, we talked about issues coming with certain accessories? I'll assume you answered "yes." Well, love comes with certain accessories but the accessories don't define *love.* In marriage, sex is something that comes with love, but sex can take place without love. Sex is an accessory; GOD is love. We mess up when we name and identify things by their accessories. Have you ever been labeled by something that you wore or something that was attached to you? Sometimes we love people based on their accessories. Example, if he can sing, he is valuable to you because you love singers. We may even create distrust for someone based on their gender; I once had a distrust for men just because they were…men. On the flip side, you could have labeled me based on my views; you could have said, "She has men problems." My issue was rejection but not trusting men was my "accessory." I'm not sure how you would have loved me though.

I don't know how the world loves me; I never figured it out; however, I took it off of my list of questions. I discovered how I loved *me.* I began to love *Jewel* for who she was….I knew who she was and I was o.k. with that. My biography is simple and concise. If you can't confess who you are, you can't confess to be anything else: Who are you? What does your biography sound like? I'll go first: I'm Jewel", born February 28th; the month of love…chocolate skin, a big smile with deep dimples on both cheeks. Jewel loves her body but she hasn't always loved it. She's not very fond of her weight but she loves the fact that she carries it well. Furthermore, she doesn't plan to carry it much longer. She works hard to stay healthy, but she tends to get frustrated when she doesn't lose weight as quickly as she had hoped to. Jewel is not over-weight because she's sick or ill…she just loves to eat. Oh yeah…Jewel is silly but can flip to a serious tone in two seconds flat. She doesn't like to play about things that aren't meant to be played with. Jewel is friendly, but don't try to befriend her too quickly because it may take her a while to connect. Don't label her as being unfriendly either, because she loves people…it just takes her a while to place them; furthermore, she does not like wasted time. Jewel will go all around the world to make a point and she loves to give examples. Nothing deep about this…this is how she learns so this how she teaches. Jewel has a tendency to instantly connect with some and she may even appear to be clingy but she loves who she loves. Jewel may walk right past you without speaking, but don't get offended; she's a deep thinker and tends to get lost in the clouds...she didn't even notice you when she walked by. Jewel doesn't like water, but she will drink it all day because it's healthy; she has a big sense of humor and tends to monitor people by their facial expressions alone, at first…a happy face is very attractive to her, but she is more likely to question a frown. This doesn't make Jewel judge you, but she will label you unapproachable if you don't smile; she will change that label when she sees more of who you are. Jewel is a social worker, called by God; this means, she will still do things God's way, within the bounds of the code of ethics. Secretly, Jewel still wants everyone to like her; spiritually, Jewel knows that's not true or healthy; she doesn't struggle with rejection but she can still identify it in her thought process. Jewel knows her strengths, she's aware of her flaws, and she works on her faults. Jewel also knows that…there is no way to sum all of "Jewel" up in one paragraph or less, but she gave you the basics. Now, that's my story; what's yours? How do you love "me"? See, the word "me" here is not just talking about *Jewel*. Me is YOU. I'm not asking you how you love ME; how do you love "you?" How would you love a person like *you?* My story may remind you of yours but how do you love YOU? I like me differently, day by day, but my love for me remains the same. If you can answer the question and are comfortable with your answer…that is great! Take it a step further; how do you respond when someone doesn't love you the way you feel they should? This can reveal some insight on how you really love you. How would you respond to rejection? This can reveal some insight on how you really love you. How would you respond to a social media subliminal message? This could reveal how you really love you. If you can answer that and you see room for improvement, fill that space with what it's worth. If you can't answer that question, I dare you to search yourself to find out how you love "me".

As for God's thoughts concerning me, God loves me! This book was written with God, my savior, in mind. See, this book was birthed from a question I asked God, during my darkest time; in return, God asked me how I loved myself. I told God all that I had done, cried out to Him and asked: "After ALL I've done and ALL that I am, how do YOU still love me? How does somebody like YOU, God, love ME?" God found a way to love me. I'm not easy to love but loving is easy for God to do; when God loves me, He is just…being Himself. I can't tell you just how much God loves me because God is still in the process of loving me and He loves me with an everlasting love. God's love is still being poured out on my life, without measure. I have not made my last mistake but He loves me as if I've never done any wrong. I can't tell you the longitude of His love because I've never measured how far the east is from the west. God's love for me supersedes any measure of hate that my worst enemy could ever express or demonstrate to me. I can't talk about how "I" love me without talking about God's love for me. I love me because I look like God. God loves me because I look like God. My life is not so much about me but…I matter to God. When I'm not sure of who I am, I can refer back to who God is. See, I don't know how you love *Jewel*; you may be still holding on to the last mistake that I made…as far as you know. The truth us, I've probably made even more mistakes since you last heard of my last one.

90

By now, you may be thinking, "Well, JEWEL, it's nice that God named you who you are but, my name is not *Jewel* so I can't use that little play on words." I agree. You may not be *Jewel but,* who are you? What does God call you? He named me Jewel but my life has been everything BUT crystal clear. My name just happens to be the "thing" that He uses to remind me of who I am. What is your "insider" when it comes to God? When we post something on social media or tag a friend, and the post is something that only the friend would know about, we might end the post with "#insider," to indicate that this "one" is between me and YOU. What is that "thing" that God uses to always bring you back to Him? What name has God given you that always reminds you of who you are? Maybe it's not your birth name; mine just happens to be. My name doesn't make me special; my identity does. My name is just an "accessory" that came with who I am and who God called me to be. What is your accessory? Find your name and only answer to who you are. You don't have to change you birth name in order to be who you were called to be.

Maybe you feel unloved or undeserving of love. I challenge you to begin your own journey, but pack lightly, my friend! The first stop will be your own mirror. Before you accept anyone else's "love", ask yourself this question and make sure that you and God have answered: "How do you love me?" Maybe, after "reading me," you feel I am undeserving of God's love; I agree. I don't know why He loves me still and chose me to be a voice for Him but He did. He won't change His mind, no matter what you think of me. I don't say this to brag; I say this because you wouldn't be the first to try to get Him to change His mind about me; I tried it long before you did and I'm telling you, God's love won't leave me…but, what does this mean for you? Everything that I've shared about how God feels about me, He feels the same for you. I'm not special…I've just received God's love for me and this makes me both valuable and a threat. I am valuable to God because I know who I am. I'm a threat to both the enemy and…anyone who doesn't know who they are. I don't take it personal either way. God will get the glory out of my life. Receiving God's love for me goes beyond the opening up of my arms; receiving God's love is being who He created me to be. Receiving God's love is more than declaring, "I love God and He loves me." We receive God's love by loving others. The word says, "IF you love me (God), keep my commandments." (John 14:15). We receive God's love by…giving love to others. John 13:34 tells us that God commands us to love one another the way that He has loved us. If we don't process God's love the right way, we might also…love people the wrong way. If God's rebuke feels like He's fussing at you, it may be easy for you to feel justified in fussing at others, in the name of "love," for example. Rebuke means to be sharp with expression and exact. Sharp also means clear; if your rebuke is laced with meanness, your point may not be clear.

Walking in Love

Let's walk through some helpful information that might help you or someone you know overcome the spirit of rejection. If you have read the entire book, you just took a journey and I'm certain that you were able to collect some jewels along the way; however, I want to leave you with some tips that will help you on your road to recovery. The first thing that you need to know is this: GOD LOVES YOU. If you've read this entire book, you might remember me stating that THIS is not just a general statement; when GOD says HE loves someone, HE is saying, "I love MY creation...I love ALL of who you are." God's love for you is not like your neighbors love for you. God created you so His love for you is the most genuine. When God says, "I love (place your name here), God is saying, I love (list some things about you) ALL of (place your name here). Yes! Even your tendency to frown when you're upset...God loves you.

Next, identify the spirit of rejection AND it's accessories. Maybe you don't deal with rejection; what do you struggle with and what accessories did that struggle come with? I won't give you a long drawn out definition that you could look up yourself, but I will give you two tips: If you can relate to my thoughts and feelings expressed in this book, you may be dealing with the spirit of rejection. If you feel you were dealt a bad hand, constantly seeking the approval of others or never satisfied with your own life and those around you, you may be dealing with the spirit of rejection. Be careful; if you are critical of others but easy on "you," you may be dealing with the spirit of rejection. If you constantly feel rejected by others and life itself, you might be dealing with the spirit of rejection. God has already accepted you and has chosen you; if you reject that truth, you could easily fall into the spirit of rejection, but not to worry...we do fall down and we get up if we don't take too much time saturating ourselves in the mud and dust. It's good to reflect on our demise, at times, but reflect from a clear stream of focus; this stream only comes from the place of a renewed mind. In order to sow a good seed to your mind, the old you must die. If you choose to lie down for a while after you fall, go ahead and... die. I'm not talking about a natural death. I'm talking about allowing a bitter seed to die...old ways of thinking. I Corinthians 15 tells us that the dead are raised again by their death; it tells us that what we sow is not made alive unless we die to it. Sometimes, we must choose to let the past go, die to it and sow a new, positive seed. Only the sewer knows what needs to be sown; no person can tell you what seeds to sow. For

93

some, we completely die and start over with new goals, new motivations, new inspirations and a new outlook on a new life. For others, we die and start over by making some things right; we may need to apologize to a few people, forgive and then walk away or stay. If we haven't gone too far to turn around, we can work with God to fix some things that we messed up or have allowed others to mess up. This could also involve mending some old broken relationships or getting closure with some things that took place in our lives. I Corinthians 15:46 also suggests to us that in sowing seeds for a new body, the natural comes first and then the spiritual. It's hard to focus on the spiritual things, like renewing your mind or getting closer to God without dealing with these natural things that may have developed as a "side effect" of your bitterness...like fear, depression or sadness. You may need to deal with your natural body and those things that may have been triggered due to your emotional state. We can rely on God because He is the Alpha and Omega...the beginning and the end; however, as I Corinthians 15: 38 suggests: "What you sow, you do not sow the body that shall be but mere grain but GOD gives it (what YOU sow) a body as He pleases, and to each seed its own body". God performs the spiritual component to our natural effort. What does it mean for God to be the "Alpha, Omega...beginning and end?" This means that not only will God be there at the beginning of your situation, but He will also have RULE of that situation from the beginning. Not only will God be there at the end of that situation, but He will have RULE at the end of that situation. God is not just present in our lives; He sits as rule over our circumstances and situations. When God says, "I will never leave nor forsake you," He is saying, "Not only will I be there, but I won't turn you over to this situation." I'm being redundant in my explanation of God's "words" because I want you to see that God does not speak idle words; God's word is so sturdy, we can stand on it. When God speaks a word, that word becomes flesh...alive. (John 1:14). When God said, "I love you," He meant to say that to YOU; it wasn't a general statement. His love for you became flesh...He gave His only son. Giving your only means, you're giving your best, the last one, the most important, run the risk of not being able to get it back, you trust the person you gave it to, you value the person you gave it to, you love that person so much, it doesn't bother you to see them with your last, etc. How does God love you? He loves you so much, He gave you the ability to love like Him.

Let's walk together, for a moment in love to talk about some key tips to overcoming the spirit of rejection:

The first step to overcoming the spirit of rejection is to learn who you are; this is often done by dismissing who you're NOT. Regardless of age, we have all, at some point in our lives, been labeled as something. It's always important to do the process of *illumination* before moving forward and then the process of elimination. Yes! The process of *illumination* is different from the process of elimination because illumination involves bringing the spot light to some situations... exposing the enemy's hand in your self-esteem. Don't think too deep though; the first person that you may have to speak the "word" to is the person in the mirror. This is the time when you search Gods word to see what He has already said about you from the beginning. This will expose every lie that the enemy has ever spoken to you concerning YOU. At this time, you will find yourself repeating scriptures like, Psalm 149:13, "I praise you (God) because I am fearfully and wonderfully made! I know that full well." NIV. This process will allow you to lay aside ever weight so you will have the strength to eliminate those things, people and places, you may have grown attached to that may be weighing you down with negativity. On the flip side, learn how to place the people you choose to keep, in the right places. For example, if you have labeled Jodie Jane as your mentor, keep her in that *seat;* don't become hurt and upset when she doesn't invite you to her personal birthday party, where she's invited people who she's labeled as friend. You labeled her and she has also labeled you. Sometimes, the person who mentors you is not your friend but they may still love you. Your friends are those persons that YOU have chosen to label as friends. These are the people who are on your level or close to it; they are the people you hang out with, go to the same places and enjoy the same things. Your mentor, however, will often times stick closer than a friend but they serve a different purpose. They have already experienced the things that you are currently experiencing and are a God sent to help you navigate through some tough times as well as enjoy the good times. Your mentor is always a few steps ahead of you which makes it a little difficult to walk together. You would either have to step it up or they would have to slow down and this would not be fair to either of you. Some mentors can be friends but some cannot. Now, this doesn't mean that you are beneath them...it only means that God sent them to you as a guide and they might be ordained to sit in the seat a few feet in front of you, so they can show you the way. It's important for you to value them and not feel some type of way towards them because you want them to be your friend. It's important to know your own value and level so you be secure in where you're "seated." You are seated in heavenly places; this means, you are seated where God wants you to be. You are not behind anyone; you are "in order." Just because you are in the company of "greatness", it doesn't mean that you are any less of a person. It only means that you are...simply in the presence of greatness.

Learn how to appreciate others but learn balance. Don't make idols of people; becoming overwhelmed with others leads us to make the accomplishments of others unobtainable for us. At times, we tend to make idols of people who were merely designed to be our partners in particular situations. I'm not talking "father-son" relationships because every child looks up to his/her father, even if the father was not always perfect. I'm speaking more of those who may possess a career path similar to ours or may presently be where we WANT to be or where we're going. We don't realize that ALL stars were made to shine. Some stars twinkle, then we have those shooting stars that most people love to capture, though they don't shoot often. Let's not forget that we also have falling stars. At the end of the night, all stars have one thing in common: they shine; this is what they were created to do. Have you ever known a person who was really talented and gifted but everybody knew it accept them? Does that sound familiar to YOU? Most of us, if we're truthful, are past the stages of knowing that there is "something" about us even if we don't think that "something" is special.

You will be amazed at how your language will change if you continue to speak the word daily, but don't just put a bible in your hand. They say that actions speak louder than words, but there is no voice that speaks as loud as your own; you may have had a hand in damaging your own self-image. It's important to realize that though you may have been rejected, you are not "a reject". You may have been raised without a father, your mother may have walked away from you at birth, but you are nobody's "reject". You were already chosen by God and the way has been prepared for you. One thing that I had to realize was that my life was the way it was because of my response to its happenings. I was not at fault for my father choosing to leave; my responses, once truth was illuminated, are what made the difference. My father walked out but I was responsible for ALL of my responses. Some of us are fortunate to have loved ones or families (of any kind…distant, God families, or church families) to embrace us and enlighten (or remind) us of what God thinks of us and this can be tricky because often times, they may choose to deal with those noticeable things, that life of living in a rejected state, has caused. Your sister or pastor may choose to tell you to get up from your pity party and do something about your state; that's not the most sensitive way to deal with a thing, but there is some truth to it. Allow the message to come through even if the messenger delivers the message in a language that is offensive to you. We are made to recognize "truth"; we know when someone is telling us something that we "need" to hear even if they don't say it the right way. For the record, the "right way" is still up in the air…however, the jury is still out on that, but who's the judge? I digress; it's important to know that you are not what you've been through, what you've seen or what you've heard. You are who God has created you to be. "Situations" already have a name: situations. Don't rename them with YOU. Although some things that you've been called may just happen to be pieces of who you are, you are only those things because God said so first.

You are not flawless, you are not perfect, you are not unlovable and you are not a "screw up," but you are responsible for decisions that you make. You are responsible, like the rest of the world, for your actions, decisions, consequences and the way you handle others during your walk. You are still wrong, at times, you are guilty, at times, and you may even be downright ugly to those who love you the most…but you are not beyond repair. You are accountable. You may be seated on the back of the row for now, but while you're there, do those things that need to be done instead of scoping out the front row to see who is, seemingly ahead of you.

Remember that you are not unworthy of salvation from God, though you may be facing some consequences that came with your decisions. Don't step out of process just because the consequences seem "ungodly". Our reactions are what takes God out of it; God does not put more on us than we can bare; if we respond to our "transformation" by rejecting those HE'S set in place to help us or if we chose to step out of process to "set some people straight", then God will have to allow us to be out of order. It doesn't mean God left you; you stepped out of line. Overcoming the spirit of rejection is an "advanced course" in God's school of life; it's like college and responding the wrong way is your choice. In grade school, we are forced to go to class and if we're not, there is a place for us…and perhaps our parents who allow it. In college, nobody has to go, show up for class or do their assignments but at the end of the course, you may be heartbroken and out of money when you don't receive your degree. "College" is not easy, but it's worth it and it's attainable…though, it's a choice.

As stated before, you are not who every man says that you are. Sure, you may discover during step one, that you are not who "they" say you are; however, it's important to admit that you may need to use some of those labels to identify those things within you that don't look like God. You may suffer with depression, which causes you to close up at times to those who love you; because of this, your loved ones might identify you as "hard to reach". This doesn't mean that you are hard to love and it doesn't mean that they have chosen not to love you. It could simply mean that getting close to you always leaves them hurting or confused about what they've done wrong when you make yourself scarce for the next two weeks after calling them one time. Don't be deceived; the word of God compels us to try every spirit, but we assume that this is our judge free ticket. This also makes you accountable and responsible for getting stuck in offense. If you are not who "they" say that you are, continue to be who you know that you are or continue your journey of seeking God to see who you are. Let's be clear: If you are caught in the "act" of stealing and are labeled as a thief, it doesn't make common sense to argue that you're not a thief in your "heart." Your heart won't change the fact that you are now identified as a thief. If you WERE a thief who decided to change his/her ways, then it still makes no sense to argue. The word tells us to do "good" and in doing so; our "doing" will silence the mouths of whisperers and doubters. (I Peter 2: 15). When you change your ways to doing good, you will silence people from talking about who you "used" to be or what you used to do. Allow your change to speak for you; your words won't carry much weight, if you've been caught in the offense before, because witnesses may still choose to carry the weight for you...and that works in your favor. You will need their "testimony" about who you "were" once God reveals who you have become! I'm glad, today, that so many saw me fall, so many saw me "crazy," and so many have already testified about who I used to be.

Now, there is a step in this process, which most people look over. During your transformation, you will need to evaluate your circle of friends. There may be a possibility that you have formed some relationships with other people who struggle with that same spirit...we're still talking about rejection. Dismantle the notion that "you all" can help each other. As I stated previously, there is no talking aloud during most tests given until you get your "grades" back. Stop talking about your story to those people who love to hear it without knowing how you came out. Delivered people, deliver people and bound people...well, they exchange stories about their "chains". Although you and Betty Joe (totally random), might have been friends since the third grade, you may need to take a step back for a while if you find that she too struggles in the same areas that you do. Maybe the step back won't be too far to keep in touch but at times, it may be necessary to completely walk away for a season or two. You may ask me, how can you know the difference? It's easy! Does Betty Joe show up for your pity party with tissue and an "empty hug"? An empty hug is that hug that you receive that may not be what you need at the time but it "feels" good; at times, you may need that friend who shows up with a box of Kleenex and a big smile, saying, "You need to get it together! I'll be here for you, but I won't help you give up!" If you have a friend who is always eager to listen and co-sign EVERY thing that you say, that is not who you need at this time. Nobody is ALWAYS right, so you know that a friend who always takes your side is not the most genuine. If they help protest your right to stay angry, bitter or depressed, then you may need to step away for a while. Does this make Betty Joe a bad friend? I don't know but that has little to do with your distancing from her. I will say that Betty Joe might be well aware of your tendency to become offended so she has decided to just listen and not "fight" with you; maybe she knows that you are not ready for the truth and would blame her if she was the one to tell you. Don't walk away with an attitude because you may need Betty Joe again; not to mention, learning how to love is one of your goals. Surround yourself with people who always seem to know your heart; these are the people who are always able to see through your motives, both good and bad, have your best interest at heart and are not afraid to love you and correct you all at the same time. These people will hurt your "feelings" at times, but they make so many positive deposits into your spirit that even when they make you angry, you know without a doubt that they are right and they want to see you win. Sometimes, these people are encouragers, while sometimes, these are the same people who will spank your bottom and wipe your tears with THEIR shirt all at the same time. Now, everyone who thinks that they can "see through you" does not always have your heart; use your spirit to discern. Identifying people wrongly could lead to major setback(s). Be careful when "cutting people off" or choosing to walk away. Don't despise the "good news" friend…the one who knows how to lift you up in your darkest hour. They know just what to say and how to say it. They speak the truth but they may leave out the rebuke. The bible says that friends show themselves friendly; however, it also says that an open rebuke is better than hidden love. (Proverbs 18:24 and Proverbs 27: 5). You can't accuse the "good news" friend of being phony because they are aware of the damage of your heart and are only trying to protect it…while praying that somebody will tell you the truth about you.

The next step is to be prepared to repeat these first six steps daily and be prepared to remind yourself daily of who you are and who you're not. Please know that while you're working while its day, other forces are working on you at "night". Sure, we have dreams and visions but this "night" time that I've mentioned, will symbolize your "dark" times. During your transformation, you will hear and see things that will remind you of your past, things that happened to you and things that you made "happen" to others; don't get stuck in offense or guilt. They will both be working, hand in hand, to destroy your progress. Your past may forever be in your memory, but your responsibility is to speak to it, tell "it" who you are and thank God that you are becoming who He's made you to be; you are no longer bound to it even if you know the way back and at times, you may feel like visiting it. It's important to know that you will have days where you feel down and need to be reminded of your progress and goals…write them down no matter how big or small they may seem to you.

Find out AND accept who you are. I can't tell you who you are, but for starters, you are the head and not the tail; this is who God made you to be; you may be the "butt of some conversations but you are not THE butt; that conversation belongs to those who are having it and head or tail, it's coming out of their mouth…not yours. God has made you to be an over comer of everything that has tried to hold you down. You are made in the image of God; you may have been rejected by men but you were chosen by God before you ever made your first mistake. It's important to know that we are forever learning more and more about ourselves each day and you shouldn't expect to learn everything about yourself overnight. Give yourself time to process things correctly. I don't know much about how food is processed, but I assume that there are only two ways to process food incorrectly: processing it too long or not enough. The same goes for your transformation. Learn to take as much time as you need to process things, but don't get stuck and process something too long…this is also called "over thinking" a thing. Truth? We can't "over-think;" What happens is, we think about it so long, that we…create a whole other scenario; now we're paranoid and imaginative, while "thinking" has long since, left the room of thoughts.

After identifying who you are, accept the facts, denounce the lies, and test everything else that hasn't been proven to decide where they fit. What I mean is, accept your "story". Your father walked out and you feel your mother should have because she wasn't there either. Accept the fact that you were raised without your father. Seek God to find out if it is necessary to gain closure or walk away while He (God) works it out for YOUR good (and He will…if you seek Him first). The facts of your life are those things that you can't change, such as your past, your complexion, the family that you were born into, or your features. Make up your

101

mind to embrace who you are and change the things that you can change and want to change. You may be insecure about your weight…you can change that. If you don't want to and you want the world to accept you the way that you are, you must, first, become comfortable with your size and embrace it. Sometimes, we don't want to work on things that we ourselves don't like, and that's our choice but we should also leave room for other's to make a choice to (or not) accept those things. You may chose not to work on the fact that you are short with people in the morning time but you continue to hurt people every morning at work. It's your choice to keep this "trait" if you feel it's just "you" but when you lose your job or when you're alienated on the job due to your "attitude", decide to also accept that as well. If you take the time to think about it, you may realize that you stay up late at night and rise early in the morning…this could mean you are cranky and sleepy and that's not your co-workers fault, neither does it mean you are not a morning person. Truth be told, you are not a night person because you cannot handle staying up at night without it ruining your morning. The object is to not allow your emotions control who you are thus forcing you to become someone else.

Make a list of things that make you who you are; I call this the list of *me*. We are forever discovering something new about ourselves, but during your transformation, your list of *me* also sets the tone for how you want others to treat you. This reminds you and says to the world, "This is how you will love me; if you can't love me this way, that's your choice but my choice is continue to only accept this type of love…a Christ like love".

During this process of learning to walk in love, the most important fact to accept is the fact that you will be rejected by someone, at some time, again…maybe even multiple times. Some days that rejection may even come from the person in your mirror. Knowing who you are really comes in handy at this point because even if you are looked over or rejected you can remind yourself that you are not a failure. You can bring to your own remembrance those areas where you have made major progress. Don't confuse *failure* with *opened doors*. See, some opened doors are also exit signs; the only difference is the sign at the top of the door…it's up to you to "not" miss it. The big door at the end of the hallway may have a big, flashing, green exit sign, but it still leads to the outside…an opened door with an opened field of possibilities. You are somebody's choice; furthermore, the ball is in your court and if it's not, that means it's not your time to catch.

A good lesson is to learn from every opportunity and always come out victorious…we do this by never giving up. The victory is found in the growth. If your heart is in it, try it again…whatever "it" is. I know that I've used the word "it" a lot but only you can identify "it." Don't seek validation from others, but accept it when it comes; this is called confirmation. Be open to correction just as much as you're opened to confirmation. Believe it or not, someone has traveled the same road that you are currently trotting.

Learn your principles and value system and don't be so easily pulled away from either of them. You may not be married, a Christian or a "saint" but everyone should start with boundaries and values…in doing so, you may discover that you are a Christian at heart, a saint and you may even be preparing to be a wife or a husband because your principles could place you in certain categories. It's easy to adopt certain principles but disown the source from whence those principles came from. Example? The world adopts principles of the bible, but disassociates those principles from Christ. The world adopts, "thou shalt not kill," but, it's often used to simply keep the world in order; the biblical sense is taken away from the principle. Biblically, we don't take a life because we are not the giver of life. In the world, you don't take a life because… we can't have people just going around killing people, now. Right? It's against the "law." As for me, my principles are found in the Bible that I choose to believe in.

Realize that it's important to separate rejection from what might have left you open to operate in it. Rejection is not what you do…it's what happens (or has happened) to you. It's important to know that rejection is the action that someone ELSE did to you; your reactions can make you take on the spirit of rejection; there is nothing deep about it…it simply means you operate as a reject and you label every no, disappointment and heart break as rejection happening to you over and over again. This is because the first offense was not properly processed. Learn to see rejection for what it is: it is what someone else decides to do to you. Your reaction should be that of a victorious person who is already confident that a closed door at the right time is a blessing! Wait in expectation for the door opened just for you, thus, once the doors swing open, you will still be standing or lying in front of the last closed door! Internalized rejection is what causes a cycle of rejection.

Last but not least, accept the fact that others have the right to choose, just as you do. People have the same options as you. Your husband or wife may choose to walk out on you and your family but that doesn't change who you have become...it only reveals their heart and they have "it" to deal with. Your assignment may be to believe God to restore your family, believe God for strength to move on, or believe God for direction, as you may not know what to do in such situation. I would love to tell you that after you change your ways, God will "make" everybody forgive you and treat you as if all things are new...but that doesn't always happen. Seek God to find out what this means to you and what position you will need to take. Somebody's life may depend on you processing things correctly, even if it's your life that's saved initially.

How do You love Me? The answer to this question is not to be taken lightly; it sets the tone for the music of your life, but don't dance yet. This question can't be answered by anyone other than you and God. Before you can ask the world this question and judge their response, keep in mind that your mirror must answer this question first.

Now, I don't want to be rude, but for now, I'll take my seat.

The whole world is listening but this time, I'll let you speak...

"How do You love ME!"

"Oh how I love me!! Let me count the ways!

With all my fingers and my toes, I'll count the ways for days!

My mirror, mirror, on the wall, you tell me what you please;

Make sure you tell me what God knows; all else, I won't believe!

My heart may grieve, with what you say, at times! I know my faults!

Remind me of my great success! Remind me of the cost!

I love you, mirror on the wall! Now how do you love ME?!

I have a feeling what you feel! Your heart resembles ME!"

Poetically Speaking,

Jewel Moore

About the Author

Author Jewel Moore, founder of *Jewel An Apple a Day,* a native of Mississippi, is an aspiring writer and friend of God. She has a passion to see people healed from those chains that are not most talked about…chains that don't make a loud noise, but weigh us down the most. Jewel's greatest passion is for those who struggle with the spirit of rejection, and every accessory that comes with the struggle. Jewel likes to consider herself, with the help of God, as the voice of reason…reminding those who feel there's no hope, God is the reason that we have hope in every issue that we may be struggling with. She obtained her BSW in Social work from the very prestigious Rust College of Holly Springs, MS. Jewel discovered a love for writing at the age of ten and began writing poetry as well as participating in several poetry slams. Jewel resides in Mississippi. Jewel is also an active member of the Delta Sigma Theta Sorority Incorporated.

Below, you will find several links to connect with Jewel Moore.

www.Authorjewelmoore@gmail.com

www.facebook.com/jewelmoorepage

www.facebook.com/jewelanappleaday

www.twitter.com/authorjewelmoore

The Beginning

Follow Jewel to keep up with her next book, coming to a bookstore near you:

"Lifting Waits"

Special Thanks:

Photography

Capturing Moments Photography

www.capturingmomentsphotography.com

Graphics

Mingo Thames II

www.facebook.com/mingothames

Design Inventions

Alyece Loyd

Justin Weatherly

www.ingramcontent.com/pod-product-compliance
Lightning Source LLC
Chambersburg PA
CBHW051840040426
42447CB00006B/626